Herbert Puchta and Jeff Stranks
with Richard Carter and Peter Lewis-Jones

English in Mind

* Workbook 3

CAMBRIDGE UNIVERSITY PRESS

CAMBRIDGE UNIVERSITY PRESS
Cambridge, New York, Melbourne, Madrid, Cape Town, Singapore, São Paulo, Delhi

Cambridge University Press
The Edinburgh Building, Cambridge CB2 8RU, UK

www.cambridge.org
Information on this title: www.cambridge.org/9780521750653

First published 2005
7th printing 2008

Printed in China by Shenzen Donnelley Printing

A catalogue record for this publication is available from the British Library

ISBN 978-0-521-75065-3 Workbook with Audio CD / CD-ROM
ISBN 978-0-521-75064-6 Student's Book
ISBN 978-0-521-75066-0 Teacher's Book
ISBN 978-0-521-75067-7 Teacher's Resource Pack
ISBN 978-0-521-75068-4 Class Cassettes
ISBN 978-0-521-54506-8 Class Audio CDs
ISBN 978-0-521-69685-2 DVD (PAL / NTSC) and Activity Booklet
ISBN 978-0-521-69684-5 VHS Video (PAL) and Activity Booklet

Contents

1 Best of British

1 Grammar

Present simple vs. present continuous review

a Complete the sentences. Use the present simple or present continuous form of the verbs.

I'm Christy Bell, and I'm in Year 11 at a school in Manchester.

This is my big GCSE exam year, so I ¹ _____don't have_____ (not have) as much free time as I did before. When I ² _____ (not do) my homework or studying for tests, I try to see my friends. Saturday night is really the only time when everyone's free, because most of my friends ³ _____ (work) on Saturdays. I have a job in a home and garden centre, but it ⁴ _____ (get) harder to find enough time to do that and all of my school work too. I ⁵ _____ (need) the money, though, because I don't get any pocket money from my mum. I ⁶ _____ (start) to do babysitting, which is good because I usually ⁷ _____ (get) my school work done at the same time (and get paid for it!).

Most of the boys in my class seem to spend a lot of their free time on computers. More and more of them ⁸ _____ (get) computer games, or doing online gaming, but I don't like them much. And these days people ⁹ _____ (use) instant messaging to talk to friends, but I ¹⁰ _____ (prefer) texting my friends on my mobile – I hate sitting in front of a computer for hours. I do enough of that with my homework.

b Put the words in order to make questions to Christy about her life. Then match questions 1–6 with answers a–f. Write a–f in the boxes.

1 not counting / how often / eat out, / school meals / do you ? ☐ *f*
  How often do you eat out, not counting school meals?

2 these days / are you / lot of / eating a / fast food ? ☐
  _____

3 and your / do you / what kind / friends listen to / of music ? ☐
  _____

4 exercise at / are you / the moment / doing much / sport or ? ☐
  _____

5 or any / do online gaming / of your / do you / friends ever ? ☐
  _____

6 your age are / think people / much money / do you / spending too ? ☐
  _____

a I'm actually in a girl's football team, and I go running two or three times a week.

b One or two of them do, but most of us think it's a stupid habit.

c They like pop and dance music. Personally I prefer rap – 50 Cent, Eminem.

d No, not really. I probably ate more burgers and chips when I was younger. I prefer salads now.

e All my friends have part-time jobs, so I think they spend just what they can afford. I buy too many clothes!

f I suppose about once or twice a month. I go to a little café in the shopping centre with my friends.

2 Vocabulary

Giving statistics and making generalisations

a Here is part of the text you heard from the Student's Book. Read it and (circle) the correct answer, a, b or c.

Britain has 12 million people under the age of 16 – around 20% of the population.

Internet fans might think British teenagers spend all their time online, but surprisingly under 10% of 15–16-year-olds have the Internet at home (just 1 in 13). However, this number is increasing all the time.

11–16-year-olds spend about £12 a week. Girls tend to spend £2 a week more than boys. In the past, this was usually spent on sweets, but now teens are spending most of their money on mobile phone cards.

If children are spending so much, that means some of them are working. The most common job is babysitting, followed by newspaper rounds.

25% of under-19s are living with just one parent.

1 .... of the population of Britain is under 16.
   a The majority   b (1 in 5)   c Just under half

2 .... teenagers are using the Internet.
   a A lot   b Over half of   c More and more

3 Teens are spending .... their money on mobile phone cards.
   a around two thirds of   b the majority of   c most of

4 It is .... teenagers to deliver newspapers.
   a quite common for   b the majority of   c about two thirds

5 .... people under 19 are living with just one parent.
   a 1 in 4   b Almost half   c It is common for

b Complete the sentences. Use the words in the box.

think	prefer	tend
common	majority	more
lot	~~half~~	

1 Almost ......*half*...... of British teenagers have cable or satellite TV <u>at</u> home.

2 Most teenagers .... seeing friends <u>to</u> watching TV.

3 Boys .... <u>to</u> play sport .... often <u>than</u> girls.

4 A .... of teenagers .... <u>that</u> going <u>to</u> the cinema is better <u>than</u> playing sport.

5 On <u>a</u> 'boring day', <u>the</u> .... <u>of</u> teenagers say they watch TV or <u>a</u> video.

6 It is quite .... for teenagers <u>to</u> have <u>a</u> part-time job.

3 Pronunciation

The schwa /ə/

a 🔊 Listen to the sentences in Exercise 2b and check your answers. How do you pronounce the <u>underlined</u> parts? Listen again and repeat.

b 🔊 Say these sentences aloud. Then listen, check and repeat.

1 Most <u>of</u> my friends tend <u>to</u> listen <u>to</u> rap.

2 <u>A</u> lot <u>of</u> my friends prefer basketball <u>to</u> football.

3 It's quite common <u>for</u> me <u>to</u> send text messages <u>to</u> my friends.

4 More <u>and</u> more teenagers <u>are</u> starting <u>to</u> use the Internet <u>at</u> home.

4 Grammar

Present perfect simple with *for*, *since*, *yet* and *already*

a Complete the sentences with *for* or *since*.

1 Pietro has been in England .... three months.
2 He has studied English .... he was seven years old.
3 His mother has been there with him .... two weeks.
4 He hasn't had any fish and chips .... he arrived.
5 He hasn't had a good cup of coffee .... he left Italy.
6 He hasn't seen his friends .... such a long time.

b Look at the pictures and write *how long* questions with short answers.

1 you know / each other?
How long have you known each other?
Since February 14th / For ...

2 she have / car?

....
....

3 you support / Newcastle United?

....
....

4 you have / watch?

....
....

c Circle the correct answer, a, b or c.

1 We .... haven't been to Scotland.
  a already b still c yet

2 I've .... come back from Stratford.
  a still b yet c just

3 But you've .... seen this film five times!
  a yet b still c already

4 Have you .... got here?
  a just b still c yet

5 I haven't had a really good ice cream ....
  a yet b just c already

6 Have you .... not been on the London Eye?
  a already b yet c still

d Rewrite the sentences using the words in brackets.

1 We still haven't had our results. **(yet)**
  We haven't had our results yet.

2 I've seen this film before. **(already)**

3 I've been doing this course for a week. **(since)**

4 Joy hasn't used her new mobile yet. **(still)**

5 I told you that a few seconds ago! **(just)**

6 You've had that computer since January 2005. **(for)**

7 Your friends still haven't called you. **(yet)**

5 Culture in mind

(a) Read about multicultural food in Britain, and match questions A-G with paragraphs 1-6. There is one question you will not need to use.

A What is Britain's favourite food these days?

B Is it only eaten in restaurants?

C How long has curry been popular in Britain?

D ~~Is fish and chips still Britain's national dish?~~

E What is 'chicken tikka masala'?

F What other 'multicultural' food is popular in Britain?

G Is curry popular just in London and other big cities?

(b) Mark the statements *T* (true), *F* (false) or *N* (not enough information).

1 Fish and chips is the oldest kind of British food still eaten today. ☐

2 'Chicken tikka masala' and 'balti' are dishes found in India, Pakistan and Bangladesh. ☐

3 The first curry house in Britain was operated by an Indian immigrant. ☐

4 London has 9,000 curry houses. ☐

5 It is possible to buy a chicken tikka masala flavoured drink. ☐

6 It is common to find British restaurants that have food from other cultures. ☐

6 Vocabulary

Making new friends

Replace the underlined words with phrasal verbs from the box.

feel left out   settled in   join in   ~~bond with~~   fit in

1 Karen's playing with her new puppy. She's trying to make an emotional connection with it.
bond with

2 What's wrong with you, Sam? Don't you want to participate in the game?

3 Have you adapted to your new environment yet, Steve? You've been here two months now.

4 I'm not going out with Harry and his friends anymore. I just don't feel like I belong.

5 Here's a present for you, Tom. I don't want you to think you're not being included.

D *Is fish and chips still Britain's national dish?*

1 Not these days. For one thing, fish is becoming more and more expensive, and our tastes seem to be changing too. In any case, fish and chips only came to Britain less than 150 years ago, so it is not really such an old traditional dish. Fish and chips was probably a mixture of French 'frites' and Jewish fish recipes.

2 Some people say it is chicken tikka masala, a British curry dish. Like 'balti', it was invented in England by Bangladeshi immigrants. The British like gravy, or sauce, with their food, and this is very different from the food you might find in India, Pakistan or Bangladesh.

3 Curry first appeared on a British menu in 1773, would you believe, so it is actually much older than fish and chips. Indian restaurants have been very popular in Britain for over thirty years. In fact, they are not really 'Indian'; most of them are operated by Bangladeshis.

4 No. You can find curry houses even in the smallest villages. There are over 9,000 of them all over Britain.

5 No, a lot of people cook their own curries at home. Sainsbury's, one of Britain's biggest supermarkets, sells 30,000 chicken tikka ready-meals a day, and you can buy chicken tikka masala flavoured crisps, pizzas, sandwiches and pasta sauce. British companies even sell it to India.

6 You can find almost anything in supermarkets these days, including 'fusion' food, which has influences from more than one culture. Afro-Caribbean food and Japanese-style sushi bars are becoming more popular in London, and you will find Chinese, Greek, Mexican and Thai food in most British towns and cities.

Skills in mind

7 Read

Read the text, and (circle) the correct answers, a, b or c.

Explosive Message

Rapper / R&B star Ms Dynamite has won many 1 _____ in her short career. She became the first black female (and youngest ever) winner of the Mercury Music Prize in 2002. Other music awards 2 _____ , and then in 2003 she won a different kind of honour – she was named Media Personality of the Year by the Commission for Racial Equality. Of course, the music prizes were very pleasing, but this one was something very 3 _____ to her.

'I'm really happy 4 _____ I've won this award. It means a lot that people are noticing that I'm fighting for something positive through my music.'

Ms Dynamite, whose 5 _____ name is Niomi McLean-Daley, is a role model for today's multicultural Britain. The songs she writes sound real

because they *are* real – her own experiences from a difficult childhood. Niomi 6 _____ born in London, but her mother is Scottish and her father Jamaican – he left 7 _____ when she was young, and her mother later became very ill for some time.

It wasn't easy growing up poor in the city. As a teenager, she had problems at school, and even left home herself for a few months when she was fifteen. 8 _____ , she still managed to get the three A-levels she needed to go to 9 _____ , but she decided to try a musical career instead. In her interviews, she often talks about the importance of education and learning about different 10 _____ . When her singing career is over, she wants to be a teacher one day.

	a	b	c	d
1	medals	money	(awards)	races
2	too	after	additionally	followed
3	special	fantastic	perfect	big
4	for	of	that	when
5	first	singer	true	real
6	is	has	were	was
7	out	house	home	wife
8	But	And	However	Although
9	school	university	work	home
10	place	cultures	country	lessons

Reading tip

Multiple choice cloze

You have already done a number of these exercises in other levels of *English in Mind*. Remember:

- It is important to think about grammar as well as meaning. In number 1, you can't say *many money*.

- Try to learn the context of a word. *Medals* and *races* are usually connected to sport.

- Learn how words can and can't combine. In number 3, it's not possible to say *very fantastic*. In number 8, only one of the choices can be followed by a comma.

- Read the whole sentence to see what kind of word is needed. In number 2, a verb is needed.

8 Write

Write a paragraph about foreign culture.

- What languages are spoken most in your country?

- Are there any famous writers, singers, actors or sports stars living in your country who were not born there?

- Choose another culture and say what you like and don't like about it.

Unit check

1 Fill in the spaces

Complete the text with the words in the box.

prize ~~emigrated~~ immigrant culture life novel watching felt settled for

The writer Kazuo Ishiguro was born in Japan, but his family ¹ _____emigrated_____ to Britain when he was five. He ² _____ in quickly to ³ _____ in England, learning the language by ⁴ _____ westerns on TV. He never really felt like an ⁵ _____ , and he loved British ⁶ _____ . He was one of the best writers on his university course. Although his first book was about Japan, he didn't visit the country ⁷ _____ many years. He ⁸ _____ more British than Japanese, so he wrote a very English ⁹ _____ , *The Remains of the Day*, which won him a major ¹⁰ _____ .

| 9 |

2 Choose the correct answers

(Circle) the correct answers, a, b or c.

1 Go and _____ in if you feel like playing.
   a stand **b** (join) **c** bond

2 We haven't eaten _____ yesterday.
   a since **b** yet **c** for

3 The _____ of my friends have a mobile phone.
   a majority **b** lot **c** half

4 British teenagers _____ to stay at school until they are eighteen.
   a like **b** tend **c** common

5 Less _____ half of my classmates have brothers or sisters.
   a under **b** of **c** than

6 You _____ haven't told me who you went out with last night.
   a already **b** yet **c** still

7 I've played the trumpet _____ I was eight.
   a when **b** since **c** just

8 My dad _____ shopping to watching football.
   a likes **b** prefers **c** thinks

9 It's OK, you're not too late. We've _____ started.
   a just **b** still **c** yet

| 8 |

3 Correct the mistakes

In each sentence there is a mistake with the present continuous / simple / perfect, or adverbs of time. Underline the mistakes and write the correct sentence.

1 How often <u>are</u> you eat out these days? *How often do you eat out these days?* _____
2 I haven't seen you since a long time. _____
3 What kind of music are you liking? _____
4 I haven't been still to the London Eye. _____
5 How long do you know your best friend? _____
6 I've been here for last week. _____
7 How much exercise you are doing at the moment? _____
8 My mother and father yet haven't come back home. _____
9 More and more people have getting broadband connections to the Internet. _____

| 8 |

How did you do?

Total: | 25 |

| ☺ | Very good 20 – 25 | ☺ | OK 14 – 19 | ☹ | Review Unit 1 again 0 – 13 |

② Ways of talking

1 Grammar
Past simple vs. present perfect simple

a Complete the dialogues. Use the past simple or the present perfect simple form of the verbs.

1 Anton: _____*Have*_____ you two
   _____*met*_____ (meet) before?
   Lauren: Yes. We both
   _____*went*_____ (go) to that party
   last week.

2 Setsuko: How long
   _____ you _____
   (know) Marek?
   Andrej: We _____ (meet)
   on the first day of this course.

3 Callum: _____ you
   _____ (see) any films
   last weekend?
   Shayla: No. I _____ (not
   go) to the cinema for ages.

4 Ramon: _____ you
   _____ (finish) that
   Harry Potter book yet?
   Tessa: Oh, yes, I _____
   (take) it back to the library
   yesterday.

5 Jay: _____ you
   _____ (speak) to Will
   yesterday?
   Soraya: No, I _____ (not
   see) him for a couple of days.

6 Carrie: _____ you
   _____ (buy) Lee's
   birthday present yet?
   Jen: Yes, I _____ (get)
   her something in town last
   night.

7 Shandra: When _____
   you _____ (learn) to
   drive?
   Jack: Me? I _____ (never
   drive) a car in my life.

8 Joe: I still _____ (not
   give) my composition in to
   the teacher.
   Kelly: Oh, I _____ (send)
   her mine by email yesterday.

b Complete the questions. Use the past simple or present perfect simple.

1 A: I've got really bad toothache.
   B: Oh, I'm sorry. How long _____*have you had it*_____ ?

2 A: We don't live in Hutton Avenue anymore.
   B: Oh, I didn't know that. When
   _____ ?

3 A: We had a great time at the cinema last night.
   B: Oh, really? What film _____ ?

4 A: I lived in Japan when I was younger.
   B: That's interesting. How long
   _____ there?

5 A: I'm working part-time in a restaurant.
   B: Oh, yeah? When _____ ?

6 A: So you've finally arrived!
   B: Sorry I'm late! How long _____
   here?

c Complete the sentences with the present simple, past simple and present perfect simple form of the verb.

①  ②

③  ④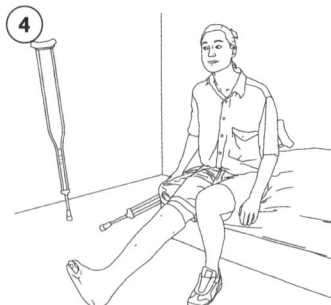

1 I _____ Pete. I _____ him for years. In fact,
   our grandfathers _____ each other when they were
   alive. (know)

2 He _____ at this restaurant since last summer. He
   _____ in the kitchen. Before that, he _____
   in a shop. (work)

3 When she was younger, she _____ in Russia. Now
   she _____ in Japan. She _____ there for five
   years. (live)

4 I _____ my leg. I _____ it on a skiing trip last
   month. I _____ something every time I ski. (break)

d Read the diary of a woman who went to a seminar to learn how to talk to animals. Some of the lines have a word that should not be there. Write the word at the end of the line, or tick (✓) if the line is correct.

I arrived here last night. Today we all paid our fee, $160 for an eight-hour	1	✓
workshop. Then we got to know our trainer, a woman ~~is~~ called Claire.	2	_is_
'I've had have horses since my childhood,' she said. 'But it took me a	3	
long while to find out that I can understand them! You can to learn this too.	4	
Animals talk all the time. You just need to learn to listen to them.' After	5	
breakfast we have worked in pairs. 'Close your eyes, think of a message	6	
and communicate it through your thoughts,' said Claire. I decided	7	
to 'tell' to my partner that 'The mountain is purple.' After two minutes of	8	
concentration (I got a headache) she told for me what she understood: 'It's	9	
too hot in here!' Well, never mind, we're here to read the thoughts of	10	
animals, not humans! After lunch, we did sat on the grass near Claire's	11	
horses and closed our eyes. Half an hour since later we went back to the	12	
house. So what messages did we have read? 'It's hot.' 'We like the grass.'	13	
Do I really need an animal communicator to learn that a horses like grass?	14	

e Two time expressions are correct, and one is incorrect. ~~Cross out~~ the incorrect answer.

1 Have you called your mother *already / yet / ~~yesterday~~*?
2 Philip has *already / just* left school *in 2004*.
3 We didn't have time to clean up *last night / already / before we left*.
4 Actually, I saw that film *two days ago / just / on Sunday*.
5 They've *never* seen snow *last winter / already*.
6 I haven't heard from Mike *since the party / for a few days / about a week ago*.
7 We had an old black Beetle *when I was little / since the 80s / for about ten years*.

f Rewrite the sentences using the words in brackets.

1 I've known Mrs Craig for four years. **(met)**
   I met Mrs Craig four years ago.
2 Jessica bought her mobile phone last week. **(for)**
3 William called a minute ago. **(just)**
4 How long have you had that bag? **(buy)**
5 Your friends have been here for an hour. **(ago)**
6 Your birthday cards got here yesterday. **(since)**
7 The last time I saw you was at your party. **(haven't)**

2 Pronunciation

Sentence stress: rhythm in questions

a Read the sentences. Underline the words that are stressed. Sometimes there is more than one possibility.

1 How long have you had it?
2 When did you move?
3 What film did you see?
4 How long did you live there?
5 When did you start working there?
6 How long have you been here?

b 🔊 Listen, check and repeat.

3 Vocabulary Body language: *say* and *tell*

a Match the two parts of the sentences. Write a–j in the boxes.

1	That guy's leaning	*i*	a	back in your chair and enjoy this film.
2	Could you try to make		b	you that warm smile when you walk in the room.
3	Just sit		c	your eyebrows at me? Is there a problem?
4	If you agree, nod		d	nervous, even if you feel it!
5	Just try to avoid		e	eye contact with the waiter? I need some water.
6	She's fantastic – she always gives		f	eye contact if you don't want to talk to him.
7	Try not to look		g	at? Do you think she's in trouble?
8	Did you just raise		h	your arms. I hope you're not getting impatient with me.
9	I see you've just crossed		i	forward a lot – do you think he's trying to listen to us?
10	What do you think she's gesturing		j	your head three times.

b Complete the sentences with the correct form of *say* or *tell*.

1 I can't _____ the difference between the new version and the old one.
2 If something is bothering you, please _____ it out loud – don't whisper to your friends.
3 He's only two years old, but he can already _____ the time.
4 Can I _____ you a secret if you promise to keep it to yourself?
5 I hope you're not _____ me a lie. You'll be in trouble if you are.
6 I'm sure you've _____ me that joke before. Don't you know any others?

c Complete the sentences with the correct form of *say* or *tell* and one of the expressions in the box.

thank you   sorry   goodbye   ~~a prayer~~   you off   him a story   the truth   that again

① 	② 	③ 	④ 
⑤ 	⑥ 	⑦ 	⑧ 

1 I've got a job interview this afternoon, so I need some luck. Will you *say a prayer* ?
2 Ouch! That really hurt! Aren't you _____ ?
3 Sorry, I didn't hear you. Could you _____ ?
4 I don't believe you! Are you sure you're _____ ?
5 That's a really nice present your gran sent you. You need to write and _____ .
6 He won't go to sleep until you _____ .
7 Well, that's the end of the class. It's time to _____ .
8 Look what you've done! Wait until your dad sees this – he's really _____ .

4 Everyday English

a Match the halves to make expressions that are used when saying *hello* or *goodbye*. Write a–e in the boxes.

1	How's		a	care.
2	Long time		b	to be going.
3	Take		c	life?
4	Nice		d	seeing you.
5	We've got		e	no see.

b Read the dialogue and (circle) the correct answers.

Zoë: Hey! Carl, is that you? Wow, long time [1]*so good / (no see) / nice seeing you!*

Carl: Hiya, Zoë. [2]*Anyway / How's things / Nice seeing you*? Are you still at school?

Zoë: Yeah, but I go to Manchester Uni in September.

Carl: Great! Are you still seeing that guy from Manchester, what's his name …?

Zoë: Kevin Riley? No, we broke up a while ago. And he's gone to London now. [3]*Anyway / All right, mate / How's things* what are you doing these days?

Carl: I'm at Liverpool Uni. That's not too far away from Manchester.

Zoë: Right! Oh, here's my bus. [4]*Take care / I've got to be / All right, mate* going. It was really nice [5]*seeing / talking / taking care of* you again, Carl.

c In each of the phrases below, write *I* for informal and *F* for formal.

1 a By the way, … ☐
   b On a separate matter, … ☐

2 a Call me if there's anything you need to know ☐
   b Please contact me if you require further information ☐

3 a Hello, how are you? ☐
   b All right mate? ☐

4 a Thank you for your reply ☐
   b It was great to hear back from you ☐

5 a I haven't heard from you for ages ☐
   b It has been some time since our last communication ☐

5 Study help

Using appropriate language

- When you learn new words and phrases, it is important to know if the language is formal or informal. For example, it is not appropriate to end a letter requesting information about a course with 'Take care'. At the same time, you can sound too formal if you write 'Yours faithfully' in an email to someone you met on a school exchange programme.

- Phrasal verbs are usually, but not always, more informal ways of saying something. It is fine to say to a friend 'Let's meet up sometime', but in a formal situation it would be better to say 'I would like to arrange an appointment for …'.

6 Vocabulary

Phrasal verbs with *up*

a Match the sentence halves. Write a–e in the boxes.

1 Look me up the next ☐
2 We could meet up this ☐
3 Guess who turned up ☐
4 I can't believe you and Tracy ☐

a have broken up!
b time you're in town.
c at the party last night?
d weekend, if you like.

b Complete the message with one of the phrasal verbs from Exercise 6a in the correct form.

Hi, Christy. I heard you and Tom have [1] .... Sorry to hear that. I hope you're not all depressed! Anyway – remember Terry, the guy who was at the drama course last summer? Well, last night he [2] .... at the café where I work. He said he'd wanted to [3] .... us .... , but he didn't know how to get in touch. I said we should all try to [4] .... sometime soon. He gave me his phone number – if you like, I could call him and we could see a film together at the weekend. Let me know.
Love, Serena

Skills in mind

7 Write

(a) Read this email to Joanne (from the photo story) from her friend Lauren.

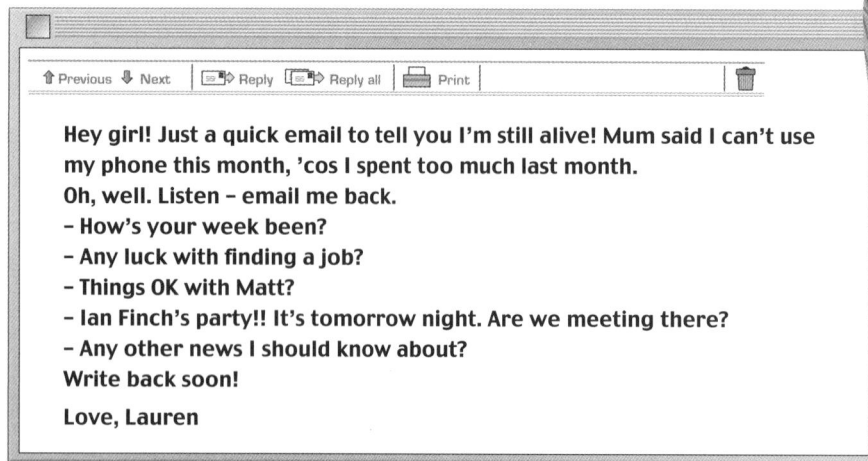

> ⬆ Previous ⬇ Next | ✉➡ Reply ✉➡ Reply all | 🖨 Print | 🗑
>
> **Hey girl! Just a quick email to tell you I'm still alive! Mum said I can't use my phone this month, 'cos I spent too much last month.**
> **Oh, well. Listen – email me back.**
> **– How's your week been?**
> **– Any luck with finding a job?**
> **– Things OK with Matt?**
> **– Ian Finch's party!! It's tomorrow night. Are we meeting there?**
> **– Any other news I should know about?**
> **Write back soon!**
>
> **Love, Lauren**

(b) Read Joanne's reply. Does she answer all of Lauren's questions? What is wrong with the underlined phrases?

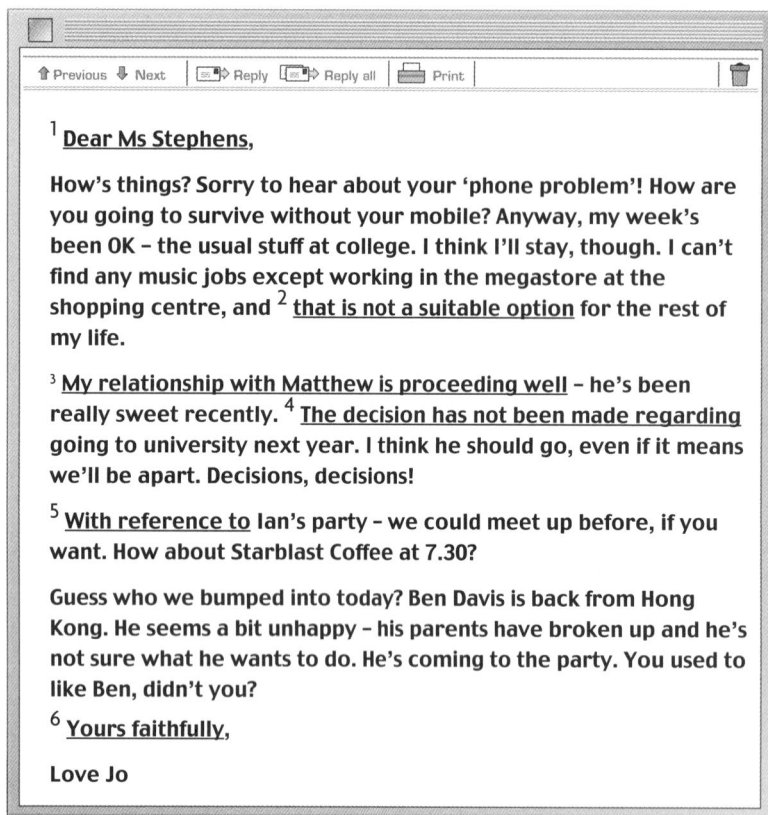

> ⬆ Previous ⬇ Next | ✉➡ Reply ✉➡ Reply all | 🖨 Print | 🗑
>
> ^{1} **Dear Ms Stephens,**
>
> **How's things? Sorry to hear about your 'phone problem'! How are you going to survive without your mobile? Anyway, my week's been OK – the usual stuff at college. I think I'll stay, though. I can't find any music jobs except working in the megastore at the shopping centre, and ^{2} that is not a suitable option for the rest of my life.**
>
> ^{3} **My relationship with Matthew is proceeding well – he's been really sweet recently. ^{4} The decision has not been made regarding going to university next year. I think he should go, even if it means we'll be apart. Decisions, decisions!**
>
> ^{5} **With reference to Ian's party – we could meet up before, if you want. How about Starblast Coffee at 7.30?**
>
> **Guess who we bumped into today? Ben Davis is back from Hong Kong. He seems a bit unhappy – his parents have broken up and he's not sure what he wants to do. He's coming to the party. You used to like Ben, didn't you?**
>
> ^{6} **Yours faithfully,**
>
> **Love Jo**

(c) Replace the underlined phrases above with phrases a–f below. Write 1–6 in the boxes.

a Things are going well with Matt ☐

b So, about ☐

c Hi, Lauren ☐

d He's still not sure about ☐

e Take care ☐

f I don't really want to do that ☐

(d) Write a similar 120-word email from Zoë to another friend using information from dialogue 4b on page 13.

Writing tip

Using appropriate language

When you write a letter or an email, it is very important to choose language that is appropriate for the reader.

- Think about who the letter is for. If it is someone you already know (a friend or a pen-friend, for example), then your language can be more simple and informal.

- Make sure you include all the information you are asked to include, in a natural way.

- When you learn new words and expressions, ask your teacher if they are formal or informal. If you learn the way to start a formal letter, also find out how to start a letter to a pen-friend, for example.

Unit check

1 Fill in the spaces

Complete the text with the words in the box.

> back   nod   make   ~~gesturing~~   telling   eye   forward   warm   look   arms

It's funny how different people communicate in groups. Some people are always ¹ _gesturing_ with their hands, and others just stand with their ² _____ crossed. Some talk non-stop, and others just sit ³ _____ and ⁴ _____ their heads occasionally. I have a problem with people who don't ⁵ _____ eye contact. When someone doesn't look at you, it seems like they're ⁶ _____ lies, especially when they ⁷ _____ nervous too. It's funny – you can give someone a ⁸ _____ smile, but they still avoid ⁹ _____ contact. It makes me want to lean ¹⁰ _____ and say, 'Hey, it's me, I'm talking to you!'

☐ 9

2 Choose the correct answers

(Circle) the correct answers, a, b or c.

1 I've _____ made a terrible mistake.
   a yet   b ever   c (just)

2 She _____ seen her boyfriend all week.
   a never   b didn't   c hasn't

3 I _____ run to college in the mornings – it's only two kilometres.
   a haven't   b usually   c didn't

4 Wait! I haven't had breakfast _____ .
   a still   b ago   c yet

5 How long _____ you wait for me last night?
   a did   b have   c do

6 I can't believe your mum didn't _____ off for taking the car without asking.
   a say you   b tell   c tell you

7 My birthday was three days _____ .
   a ago   b just   c last

8 My brother and sister _____ bought me a present for my birthday.
   a didn't yet   b has never   c still haven't

9 You haven't _____ sorry for shouting at me.
   a say   b saying   c said

■ 8

3 Correct the mistakes

In each sentence there is a mistake with the tense or time reference. Underline the mistakes and write the correct sentence. Sometimes there is more than one way of correcting.

1 How long <u>did</u> you <u>known</u> them?   *How long have you known them?* **or** *How long did you know them?*

2 I haven't finished reading it just. _____

3 I've seen that film yesterday. _____

4 Where were you been? _____

5 He's had that computer since ten years. _____

6 I live here for six months – and I love it! _____

7 Have you yet had a shower? _____

8 The coffee shop has closed two hours ago. _____

9 I never taken photos with a digital camera. _____

■ 8

How did you do?

Total: ☐ 25

| ☺ | Very good 20 – 25 | ☺ | OK 14 – 19 | ☹ | Review Unit 2 again 0 – 13 |

③ A true friend

1 Grammar

Past simple vs. past continuous review

(a) Choose the correct space for the words in brackets.

1 .... I dropped my money
    while I was running home. (while)

2 .... we got to school ....
    there was smoke coming from the science
    block. (when)

3 .... they were fighting ....
    we escaped through the back door. (while)

4 .... I thought it was good
    .... I was watching it but now I'm
    not so sure. (while)

5 .... people were crying
    .... the film finished. (when)

6 .... I knew I had done something
    silly .... everyone started laughing.
    (when)

(b) Complete the sentences with the past simple or past continuous form of the verbs.

1 While I _was looking_ (look) for my tennis
   balls, I _found_ (find) an old sandwich
   under my bed.

2 When my parents .... (come) back,
   we .... (have) a party.

3 When I .... (open) the door, they
   .... (dance) in the dark.

4 I .... (find) this girl's phone number
   while I .... your room (clean).

5 While we .... (wait), we
   .... (start) to write the invitations.

6 I .... (teach) a gym class when I
   .... (hear) about the plane crash.

7 Someone .... (call) you on your
   mobile while you .... (take) the dog
   for a walk.

(c) Complete the sentences with the past simple or past continuous form of the verbs.

Godzilla the cat has a special relationship with her
owner, David White. In the past, David often
[1] _went_ (go) away to work, and his parents
[2] .... (come) to the house in Oxfordshire,
England, to look after the cat. When David
[3] .... (call) home, Godzilla [4] ....
(run) and sat next to the phone as soon as it
[5] .... (start) ringing, his parents said. 'When
other people [6] .... (call), the cat wasn't
interested. But somehow she [7] .... (seem)
to know that David [8] .... (call).' David is
convinced he has a special bond with his cat. The calls
were always at different times of the day, and Godzilla
[9] .... (not respond) to David's voice because
she got to the phone while it [10] .... (still ring).

(d) Connect the sentences with the words in brackets.
Sometimes you need to change the order of the
sentences.

1 His parents came to stay at his house. David went
   away to work. (when)
   When David went away to work, his parents
   came to stay at his house.

2 The phone started ringing. Godzilla ran and sat next
   to the phone. (as soon as)

3 The hall light came on. She was parking her car. (as)

4 The dog started barking. I got to the gate. (as soon as)

5 Sometimes an animal starts behaving strangely.
   Something happens to its owner. (then)

6 Many animals are waiting at the door. Their owners
   are still travelling home. (as)

2 Pronunciation

Linking sounds

(a) Look at the way these words from Exercise
1c are linked:

her   owner
David   often
went   away
look   after

(b) 🔊 Mark similar links in the text, then
listen and check.

3 Grammar

Past simple vs. past perfect simple

(a) Match the sentence halves. Write a–d in the boxes.

1 A man was arrested for a bank robbery after police called him on his mobile phone. The man ...

2 A man was arrested in hospital for trying to steal money from a house safe after police found his glove at the house. The safe ...

3 A man who had climbed Mount Everest six times died as a result of a fall at home. He ...

4 An unemployed man who tried to print his own money was caught as soon as he tried to spend it. He ...

a had used black ink on the notes instead of green, because he was colour-blind.

b had left a business card at the bank with his phone number on it.

c had fallen on his hand and cut off one of his fingers. The man ran away, leaving his glove behind. When the man went to hospital with a missing finger, the police were able to match the finger to the hand.

d had climbed a ladder to change a light bulb in the kitchen when he fell and cracked his head on the sink.

(b) Complete the sentences. Use the past perfect and the past simple or past continuous forms of the verbs.

1 As soon as he _____ (close) the door, he _____ (realise) that he _____ (leave) his key inside.

2 I _____ (have) the feeling that I _____ (meet) her somewhere before.

3 I _____ (not know) what I _____ (say) to her, but she _____ (cry).

4 They _____ (get) to the cinema ten minutes after the film _____ (start).

5 My mobile _____ (not work) because I _____ (forget) to charge it.

6 I _____ (see) you sitting and smiling half an hour before the end of the exam. _____ you already _____ (finish)?

(c) Read the text about the American TV show *Friends*. Some of the lines have a word that should not be there. The problems are connected to tenses. Write the incorrect extra word at the end of the line, or tick (✓) if the line is correct.

Friends is still ~~being~~ one of the most popular TV shows in the world,	1 *being*
even after they stopped making it in 2004. The show had had three	2 ✓
previous names before it had became simply *Friends*: *Friends Like Us*,	3 _____
Across The Hall and *Six Of One*, but in the end one word was been	4 _____
enough. Apart from the main six characters, the only other person to	5 _____
appear in all ten years that they have made the show was Gunter, the	6 _____
coffee shop server. He was having the only person in the cast that knew	7 _____
how to operate a cappuccino machine.	
Why was the show so popular? It was being usually well written and	8 _____
funny, of course, but what has kept fans watching for more than a decade	9 _____
is possibly the fact that the group of six always did stayed friends, no	10 _____
matter what were problems the characters had on screen, or the actors	11 _____
had in real life.	

4 Vocabulary

Friends and enemies

(a) Replace the underlined words with a phrase from the box. Write a–f in the boxes.

> a let me down   b fallen out   c ~~tell on me~~   d stand by you   e get on well with
> f sticking up for me

1 Please don't <u>tell anyone that I did it</u>! I'll be your friend forever! — [c]

2 Your most loyal friends are the ones who <u>stay loyal to you</u> in the bad times. — [ ]

3 Thanks for <u>supporting me</u> in there. I thought nobody was going to agree with me. — [ ]

4 You really <u>have a good relationship with</u> your stepbrothers and stepsisters, don't you? — [ ]

5 It looks like Darren and Varsha have <u>stopped being friends</u>. They don't talk to each other anymore. — [ ]

6 You said you would go with me! Please don't <u>disappoint me</u> – I don't want to go alone. — [ ]

(b) Choose a phrase from the box above to complete sentences 1–5 below. Write a letter in the spaces. There is one phase you will not need.

(1)

(2)

(3)

(4)

(5)

1 Oh, no! What have I done? Look, don't _____ and I'll give you some of my sweets.

2 It's amazing that they _____ each other.

3 Come on, come on! Please don't _____ now!

4 Phew! Thanks for _____ .

5 Oh no, it looks like they've _____ with each other. Be careful what you say.

5 Fiction in mind

For over fifty years, Charlotte's Web has delighted readers around the world. Set on a farm, it is the story of a great friendship between Charlotte, a very intelligent spider, and Wilbur the pig. Charlotte does everything she can to stop Zuckerman the farmer from killing the pig – not an easy thing on a farm. The story is especially remarkable for the way it teaches children how to deal with death in a positive way. This extract introduces Charlotte's first 'miracle', as she tries to convince the farmer that Wilbur is a genius.

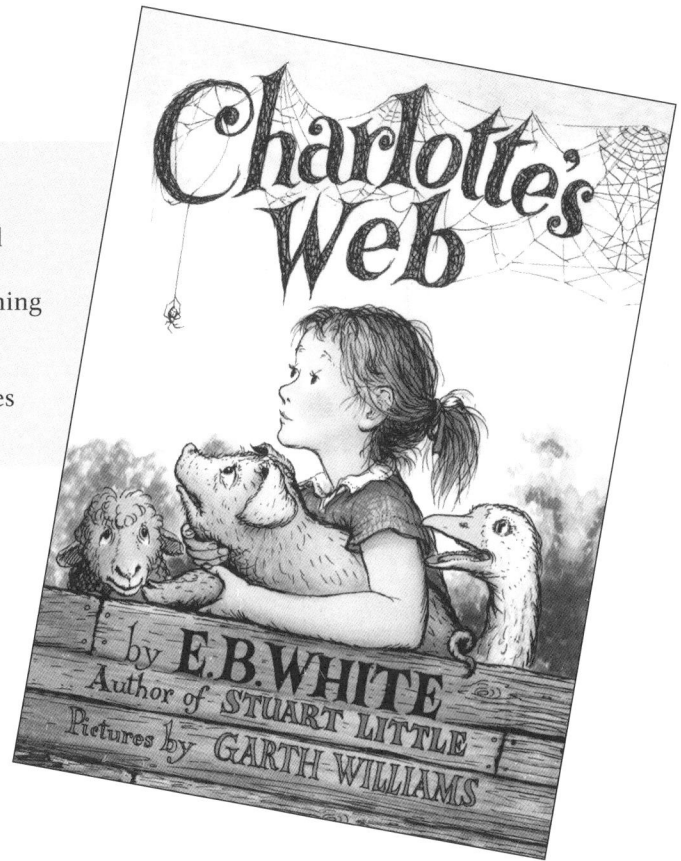

a Read the text and circle the correct word, a, b or c which is closest in meaning to the numbered words in the text.

1	a line	b grass	c wall
2	a cups	b drops	c glasses
3	a shone	b moved	c broke
4	a body	b container	c spider
5	a wrote	b read	c said
6	a shake	b cry	c laugh
7	a sleep	b work	c fun

THE MIRACLE

The next day was foggy. Everything on the farm was dripping wet. The grass looked like a magic carpet. The asparagus patch looked like a silver forest.

On foggy mornings, Charlotte's web was truly a thing of beauty. This morning each thin [1] strand was decorated with dozens of tiny [2] beads of water. The web [3] glistened in the light and made a pattern of loveliness and mystery, like a delicate veil. Even Lurvey, who wasn't particularly interested in beauty, noticed the web when he came with the pig's breakfast. He noted how clearly it showed up and he noted how big and carefully built it was. And then he took another look and he saw something that made him set his [4] pail down. There in the centre of the web, neatly woven in block letters, was a message. It said: SOME PIG!

Lurvey felt weak. He brushed his hand across his eyes and stared harder at Charlotte's web.

'I'm seeing things,' he whispered. He dropped to his knees and [5] uttered a short prayer. Then, forgetting all about Wilbur's breakfast, he walked back to the house and called Mr Zuckerman.

'I think you'd better come down to the pigpen,' he said.

'What's the trouble?' asked Mr Zuckerman. 'Anything wrong with the pig?'

'No – not exactly,' said Lurvey. 'Come and see for yourself.'

The two men walked silently down to Wilbur's yard. Lurvey pointed to the spider's web. 'Do you see what I see?' he asked.

Zuckerman stared at the writing on the web. Then he murmured the words 'Some Pig'. Then he looked at Lurvey. Then they both began to [6] tremble. Charlotte, sleepy after her night's [7] exertions, smiled as she watched. Wilbur came and stood directly under the web.

b Answer the questions with *T* (true), *F* (false) or *N* (not enough information).

1 It was probably not summertime. ☐
2 Lurvey came to feed the spider. ☐
3 Lurvey didn't see the spider's web. ☐
4 The men discovered that the pig was sick. ☐
5 Zuckerman was happy to see the words on the web. ☐
6 Charlotte had probably worked all night on the web. ☐

Skills in mind

6 Listen

a ◁)) Read the statements below, then listen and read what the person says about pets and their owners. Decide which statement you think is the speaker's opinion.

A Pet owners have a special understanding with their animals.

B Only dogs have a telepathic relationship with their owners, not other pets.

C The 'special relationship' between a pet and its owner does not really exist.

'A lot of people seem to think that pets, especially dogs, are somehow telepathic. They think that they have a special understanding with their animal, so that for example their pet knows when they are coming home, or knows when something is wrong. I think that's ridiculous, though. These things are just coincidence, or it's just that the owner is trying to 'wish' that their pet is special.'

The speaker says 'A lot of people seem to think ...', but this probably does not include the speaker. The speaker also says 'especially dogs', which does not mean only dogs. The third and fourth sentences give the speaker's opinion: 'I think ...'. The correct answer is 'C'.

b ◁)) Listen to five people talking about best friends, and match each speaker with one of the options A–F. Use each letter only once. There is one extra letter you do not need to use.

Speaker 1 ☐

Speaker 2 ☐

Speaker 3 ☐

Speaker 4 ☐

Speaker 5 ☐

A It's not necessary to see your best friend every day.

B You don't always like people the first time you meet them.

C Some people don't have any friends.

D It's not important to have a 'best' friend.

E It's not so hard to make 'new best friends'.

F It's normal to fight with your best friend sometimes.

Listening tip

Matching speakers with opinions

In this kind of question, you will usually hear a number of different people talking about a similar subject.

- It is important to read the statements carefully first, to be clear about the differences between each one.

- The speakers may use different words from the ones in the statements, but the idea will be the same.

- Try to think of other ways to express the ideas in the statements, to imagine what the speaker might say. For example, when the statement is 'It's not necessary', the speaker might say 'You don't have to' or 'You don't need to'.

- The speaker may seem to be agreeing with the statement because they use the same words, but actually go on to disagree with the statement and therefore think the opposite. For example, the speaker might say, '*Some people* think you have to see your best friend every day, *but I don't* think that's necessary.'

- Remember you are being asked for *the speaker's* opinion, not yours!

Unit check

1 Fill in the spaces

Complete the text with the words in the box.

loyalty ~~friendships~~ up out stood get letting had While friends

One of the great [1] _friendships_ in literature is the one between the hobbits Frodo Baggins and Samwise Gamgee in *The Lord of the Rings*. Sam, who [2] _____ been Frodo's servant at their home in the Shire, accompanied Frodo and his company on a journey to destroy the ring and save the world. [3] _____ they were making their journey, Sam [4] _____ by his master through all kinds of danger, never [5] _____ him down. The story shows us that, even for people who [6] _____ on very well, there are times when our [7] _____ is tested and we can fall [8] _____ with each other. However, true [9] _____ always stick [10] _____ for each other in the end.

[9]

2 Choose the correct answers

(Circle) the correct answers, a, b or c.

1 You're not going to tell _____ her, are you?
   a well   b down   c (on)

2 Her old car never _____ her down.
   a makes   b does   c lets

3 _____ soon as we left, the snow started.
   a While   b As   c Then

4 I _____ already bought my tickets for the show before we got to the theatre.
   a have   b was   c had

5 Dogs are very _____ to their owners.
   a loyal   b friend   c stick

6 While she was having a shower, somebody _____ her towel.
   a stole   b had stolen   c was stealing

7 _____ my brother was born, we moved to a bigger house.
   a While   b When   c Then

8 My best friend and I fall _____ about twice a week, but we're soon friends again.
   a up   b out   c in

9 I _____ want to watch the film because I had seen it three times before.
   a hadn't   b didn't   c wasn't

[8]

3 Correct the mistakes

In each sentence there is a mistake with past tenses or time conjunctions. <u>Underline</u> the mistakes and write the correct sentence.

1 I called you <u>while</u> I heard the news.   *I called you as soon as I heard the news.*

2 My brother and I wasn't going out until you called. _____

3 I hadn't meet your friend before last night. He's very nice. _____

4 We were so late that the show already started. _____

5 We got here as soon we could. _____

6 I realised that I left my money at home. _____

7 Were you already been here before last year? _____

8 It was sunny and the birds were sung. _____

9 I hurt my leg while I had played football. _____

[8]

How did you do?

Total: [25]

| 😊 | Very good 20 – 25 | 😐 | OK 14 – 19 | 😞 | Review Unit 3 again 0 – 13 |

④ A working life

1 Grammar

Present perfect simple vs. present perfect continuous review

a ⓐ Circle the correct words.

1 Your brother has (written) / *been writing* three job applications this morning.
2 I've *been doing / done* an IT course at the weekends. I've got one more week to go.
3 I don't leave school for another year, but I've already *started / been starting* to look for a job.
4 Have you *seen / been seeing* the new Bond film?
5 My dad has always *had / been having* a thick beard.
6 What do you mean, you haven't had time to make dinner! What have you *done / been doing* all evening?
7 It's *snowed / been snowing* all night. Do you think it'll stop by tomorrow morning?

b Complete the sentences with the words in the box.

> gone   ~~been going~~   called   been calling   taken   been taking   painted   been painting

1 Her French is getting much better. She's _been going_ to classes twice a week.
2 I've _____ three of the walls and both doors – just one more wall to go.
3 You've just _____ me! Did you forget to tell me something?
4 He's _____ out, I'm afraid. If you want to wait, he'll probably be back in an hour.
5 I've _____ photos for the last two hours. I don't have any film left now.
6 Have you _____ in here? It certainly smells like it.
7 Alisha's _____ you all day. Where have you been?
8 Who has _____ the last piece of cake? I wanted it!

c Complete the dialogues. Use the present perfect simple or continuous.

1 A: Do you want a slice of this pizza? It's excellent.
   B: No, thanks. I've just
   _____ . (eat)
2 A: Sorry I'm late! How long
   _____ ? (wait)
   B: Since two o'clock.
3 A: What _____ ? (do)
   B: Helping Dad change a tyre on the car.
4 A: Where's your sister?
   B: She _____ . (go)
5 A: _____ (finish)
   cleaning up in there?
   B: No, not yet.
6 A: You look terrible! What's wrong?
   B: Oh, I _____ (not
   sleep) well recently.

d Complete the questions. Use a verb from the box in the present perfect simple or continuous form.

do   have   ~~go~~   download   save   know

1   So is that your new boyfriend? How long
    have you been going _____ out with him?

2   Nice sweater, Jake. How long _____ it?

3   I didn't know you could water ski! How long
    _____ that?

4   I hear you want to buy a new sound system. How
    long _____ for it?

5   You didn't tell me you'd passed all of your exams!
    How long _____ ?

6   That mp3 file is huge! How long _____ it?

e Continue the paragraph about British singer/ songwriter Craig David using the information below. Use past simple and present perfect simple or continuous where appropriate.

- born 1981 in Southampton, England
- started singing and DJing at age 14
- first number 1 hit in April, 2000
- won various music industry awards since then
- also recorded his song *Rise And Fall* in Panjabi
- met Nelson Mandela

Craig David was born in Southampton, England, in 1981. He has been ...

2 Grammar

had better / should / ought to

a Circle the correct words in these sentences.

a   You'd (better) / should / ought do it before Mum comes home!

b   You *ought / better / shouldn't* play with matches.

c   You *ought not / better not / shouldn't* to let him use the Internet.

d   You *better / should / ought* talk to some of your teachers about it.

e   You'd *should / better / ought* wear some smarter clothes. You're always so untidy!

f   You *ought / should / better* to look at the advertisements in the paper.

g   You'd *ought / better / should* not get back after midnight.

b Match the problems below with the advice in Exercise 2a. Write the letters a–g in the boxes.

1   'I'm going to get home late tonight.'   `g`

2   'I've burnt my fingers.'   ☐

3   'I want a better job.'   ☐

4   'I've got an interview for a job.'   ☐

5   'I don't know what career I want.'   ☐

6   'I haven't tidied up my bedroom yet.'   ☐

7   'My son spends all night in chat rooms'.   ☐

c Read the notes of Ron Belcher's doctor, and write sentences to complete the doctor's advice. Use *should / ought to / had better* (positive or negative forms) at least once each.

- smokes 40 cigarettes a day – high cancer risk
- drinks four litres of coca-cola a day – terrible for stomach
- orders take-away food every night – awful diet
- watches eight hours of TV a night – the man's a vegetable
- drives everywhere – no exercise at all

Mr Belcher

I'm afraid you might have to make some changes to your lifestyle if you want to live to be 40. First of all, I think you'd better ...

Pronunciation

/ɔː/ *short*

(a) There are twelve words on page 23 that have the sound /ɔː/. Can you find them all? Don't repeat the same word, and don't include *for* (because this does not have the same sound in the example on page 23).

(b) 🔊 Listen to the twelve words, and repeat.

4 Vocabulary

Jobs and work

(a) Complete the crossword by solving the clues with words from page 27 of the Student's Book.

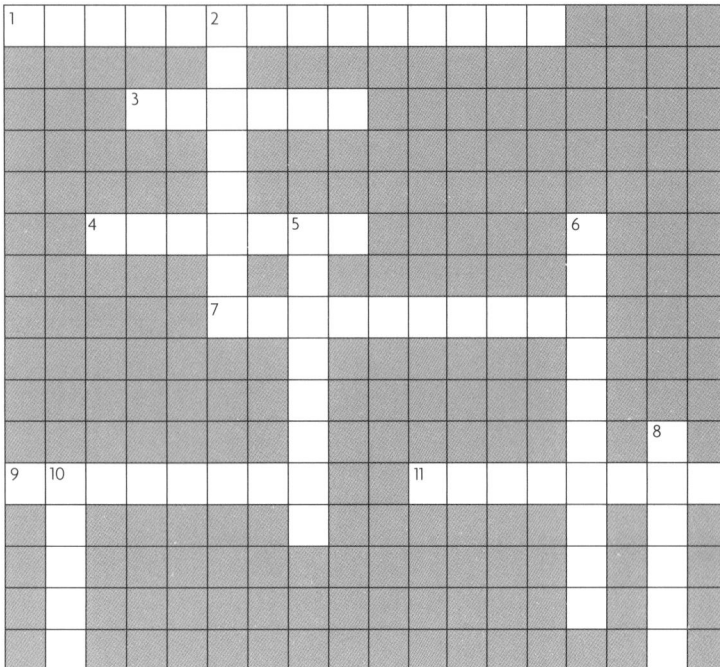

Across

1 You can get them from school and university (14)
3 This is your money from work (6)
4 Someone who is learning the skills of a job (7)
7 You have this if you've done the job before (10)
9 Not working all of the working week (4-4)
11 The one you work for (8)

Down

2 Working the complete week (4-4)
5 A worker for a company (8)
6 Without a job (10)
8 Leave a job (6)
10 Try to get a job (5)

(b) Complete the dialogue with words from the box.

> salary   ~~qualifications~~   applied
> employer   employees

Interviewer: Well, Ms Lane, I see you have a degree in mechanical engineering and a Masters in physics. Those are very impressive ¹ *qualifications* . Why have you ² _____ for a job with us?

Ms Lane: I think you're a very fair ³ _____ . You treat your ⁴ _____ very well from what I hear. And the ⁵ _____ is excellent for a first job.

(c) Complete the dialogue with words from the box.

> ~~full-time~~   part-time   resign
> trainee   unemployed

Job Shop Officer: Are you in ¹ *full-time* work at the moment, Alan?

Alan: No, I'm not working at all. I've been ² _____ for the last two weeks.

Job Shop Officer: Did you ³ _____ from your previous job?

Alan: Yes, I did.

Job Shop Officer: What happened? You were in your first month as a ⁴ _____ , weren't you?

Alan: Yes, but the training programme was very poor.

Job Shop Officer: Well, at the moment the only job we have in your field is ⁵ _____ – mornings, Monday to Friday, twenty hours a week. Do you think you would be interested in that?

5 Culture in mind

a) Read more about The Byrds and The Monkees, and why the song *So You Want to Be a Rock 'n' Roll Star* was written. Some sentences are missing from the text. Complete the text with the sentences a–f below. There is one sentence you will not need.

In the mid-1960s, as **The Byrds** were becoming one of the biggest bands in the USA, the traditional way to the top of the music business was through hard work.
1 _____

Then things started to change. After the success of The Beatles' film *A Hard Day's Night*, TV producers in the USA decided to 'create' a band especially for a TV show.
2 _____

Only one of the four band members was actually a musician. They didn't write their own songs, and even some of their music was performed by other people. But this didn't stop them from being very successful.
3 _____

Roger McGuinn and Chris Hillman, songwriters for The Byrds, felt they had to write a song about this new phenomenon of manufactured bands – the first time someone had made fun of the rock 'n' roll business in this way.

The TV show lasted only two years. The Monkees, perhaps tired of people saying they weren't a real band, learned how to write and perform their own music, but still broke up a year later.

Now, forty years on, the charts are full of manufactured bands. TV talent shows have produced a large number of instant stars.
4 _____

Some, like The Monkees, learn how to write songs, play instruments and even sing.
5 _____

Now, forty years after it was written, *So You Want to Be a Rock 'n' Roll Star* is still very relevant.

a But others disappear after their first hit song.
b A band had to know how to write songs, and how to play instruments.
c Winners of these shows are guaranteed to make the charts.
d Electronic music became even more popular in the 1980s.
e At one point, The Monkees sold even more records than The Beatles.
f This band was called The Monkees.

b) 🔊 Listen to Abby talking about a live pop concert she went to in Dublin, Ireland. Complete the notes with one or two words while you listen.

1 Abby thought the concert was probably ___*the best*___ she had seen.
2 She thought that Girls Aloud was the best group. She was _____ by how good they were.
3 *Mars Attack* and *Boogie Down Love* were her favourite _____ .
4 The sound quality in the theatre was good for Abby because she sat _____ .
5 She agreed that the tickets _____ .
6 Luke Thomas was a singer that Abby _____ .
7 The concert made €250,000 for a _____ charity.

Skills in mind

6 Listen and write

a 🔊 Listen to Chris describing a concert he saw, and complete the missing information.

Introduction
This report will describe a live event I attended recently. The event was a pop concert featuring ¹_____ different singers and bands. Some of the money from ²_____ sales was given to charity for people with physical and mental disabilities.

Venue and cost
The concert ᵃtook place at the M.E.N. Arena in Manchester. Tickets were ³_____ , depending on where the seats were.

Atmosphere
At the beginning of the show, the sound wasn't ⁴_____ . Later, the quality improved a lot. The lighting was very impressive. The crowd was very young; the average age was probably about ⁵_____ .

Performances
Most of the performers played ⁶_____ songs. There were some delays between performances. Blue were the main band; they played last. I thought Craig David was the best performer; his singing and dancing were excellent, and the audience responded very well.

Conclusion
ᵇTo sum up, the show was ⁷_____ long, which was ᶜgood value for money. Not all performers were equally good, though, and perhaps it would be a good idea to cut the number of performers. This show is touring the country, and my recommendation is that, if you like just two or three of the artists, you should definitely go and see it. ᵈOverall, it was an excellent evening, with something for everyone.

b Match the underlined words and phrases a–d with phrases 1–4 below.

1	all in all ☐	3	was held ☐
2	in conclusion ☐	4	well worth it ☐

c Your class is doing a survey on live events that they have attended (music concerts, dance and theatre performances, craft fairs, sports etc.). Write a report of 120–150 words about a live event you have seen, including information about where the event was held, the cost, a general description, what you liked and did not like about it, whether other people might like it, and a recommendation as to how the event could be better in some way.

Unit check

1 Fill in the spaces

Complete the text with the words in the box.

| part-time | for | should | been | work | ~~job~~ | qualifications | experience | trainee | employee |

Everybody keeps asking me what kind of [1] _____job_____ I want to do when I leave school. My mum doesn't think I [2] _____ apply [3] _____ any jobs yet. She wants me to go to university and get some good [4] _____ so that I can be a teacher. My dad wants me to start [5] _____ for his bank as a [6] _____ . He says I could do the job [7] _____ to get some [8] _____ , and go to college on my days off. I don't know if I want to be an [9] _____ of a bank, though. I've [10] _____ thinking about maybe trying to sell some of my art. Decisions, decisions!

9

2 Choose the correct answers

Circle the correct answers, a, b or c.

1 How long have you been _____ ?
   a resigned   b (unemployed)   c promoted

2 I really think you'd _____ say sorry before it's too late.
   a should   b ought   c better

3 How long have you _____ waiting for me?
   a just   b had   c been

4 Why don't you _____ for that job? You might get it.
   a apply   b trainee   c employee

5 _____ she be doing that?
   a Has   b Should   c Had

6 It looks like she _____ been crying.
   a has   b just   c have

7 She's a good _____ and I like working for her.
   a employee   b women   c employer

8 I didn't get the job as I don't have enough work _____ .
   a trainee   b experience   c qualification

9 When do you think we _____ to tell them we're leaving?
   a ought   b should   c better

8

3 Correct the mistakes

In each sentence there is a mistake with the present perfect or *should / ought to / had better*. Underline the mistakes and write the correct sentence.

1 <u>Shouldn't</u> you better call them back?   *Hadn't you better call them back?*

2 Our TV hasn't working very well recently. _____

3 Hi, Mum! Can you believe I've been lost my keys again? _____

4 Do you think I had sell my computer? _____

5 My friends hasn't been emailing me. I wonder what's wrong?

_____

6 At last! We've been tried to reach you all morning. _____

7 You're not well. You ought take some time off. _____

8 Have you cried? Your make-up looks funny. _____

9 You should better not tell anyone – it's a secret. _____

8

How did you do?

Total: [25]

| 😊 | Very good 20 – 25 | 😐 | OK 14 – 19 | 😞 | Review Unit 4 again 0 – 13 |

5 Travel

1 Grammar

Future review

a Complete the sentences. Use a verb from the box and the correct form of *going to*.

> sneeze   play   break   do
> be   ~~rain~~   crash   start

1 It *'s going to rain* .

2 We _____ tennis.

3 I _____ .

4 She _____ sick.

5 They _____ .

6 He _____ his homework.

7 It _____ .

8 You _____ it.

b Look at Martin's diary and write sentences about his plans for next week.

Tuesday	– morning drive to Glasgow – afternoon have a meeting with Jake
Wednesday	– morning drive back to Manchester – afternoon play squash with Andy
Thursday	– morning fly to Madrid – evening have dinner with Carlos and Conchita
Friday	– afternoon go back to Manchester – evening take Julie to cinema

1 On Tuesday morning he *'s driving to Glasgow.*
2 On Tuesday afternoon he _____ .
3 On Wednesday morning he _____ .
4 On Wednesday afternoon he _____ .
5 On _____ .
6 On _____ .
7 On _____ .
8 On _____ .

c Complete the dialogue. Use the verb in brackets and a form of *will*.

Travel agent: So, here's an idea for your holiday – Sri Lanka. If you go there, I'm sure you ¹ _will have_ (have) a good time.

Mrs Jones: Mmm. It looks nice in the photo. But we want lots of sunshine. ² _____ we _____ (get) rain if we go there in January?

Travel agent: No, it hardly ever rains in January! So, don't worry, it ³ _____ (not rain) – well, not very much.

Mrs Jones: What about hotels? Where can we stay that's nice?

Travel agent: Well, there's a lovely place called the Plaza Sun, in Colombo. You could *try* lots of other places – but you ⁴ _____ (not find) a better hotel than this one.

Mrs Jones: Is it near the beach?

Travel agent: Not far. It's in the town centre, so you ⁵ _____ (not have) a view of the sea. But it's very quiet, and very comfortable – I think you ⁶ _____ (like) the hotel a lot.

Mrs Jones: OK. But tell me – what's the food like in Sri Lanka?

Travel agent: Well, the food there is quite different – spicy, but it's delicious and not expensive.

Mrs Jones: My husband ⁷ _____ (not like) that – he doesn't like spicy food.

Travel agent: Well, I'm sure you ⁸ _____ (find) some restaurants that serve European food.

Mrs Jones: Well, I'm not sure. I think perhaps we should stay in Europe.

d Read the sentences. Mark *A* if it is an arrangement; *P* if it is a prediction; *I* if it is an intention.

1 I've decided on a subject to <u>study</u> at university – Biology. | *I*

2 <u>We've</u> arranged to <u>visit</u> my grandparents on Saturday. | ☐

3 <u>My dad</u>? <u>Give</u> me money to buy a new computer? Definitely not! | ☐

4 <u>I</u> phoned the doctor and made an appointment to <u>see</u> her tomorrow morning. | ☐

5 <u>Planes fly</u> from London to Australia in ten hours in the future? Yes, definitely. | ☐

6 <u>My friend Mike</u> has decided to <u>leave</u> school next year. | ☐

e Use the <u>underlined</u> words in Exercise 1d to make sentences.

1 *I'm going to study Biology at university.*

2 _____

3 _____

4 _____

5 _____

6 _____

2 Pronunciation

/ɡənə/ *going to*

a 🔊 Listen to the sentences. Circle where you hear *gonna*. <u>Underline</u> where you hear *going to*.

1 They're going to have a party.
2 They want me to go, but I'm not going to.
3 My dad's going to be really angry!
4 Are you going to watch the match tonight?
5 I don't want to watch it. Are you going to?
6 We're going to have a test tomorrow.

b 🔊 Listen again and repeat the sentences.

3 Vocabulary

Travel

(a) Unscramble the words and write them under the pictures.

| opmtflar | sucmost | glifth | emitbleat | usecir | beaggga | roadgnib rdac | prureadet ulogen |

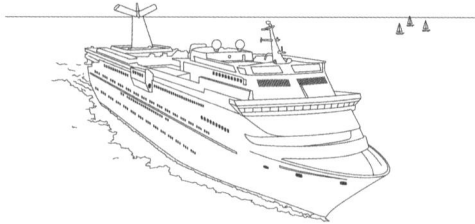

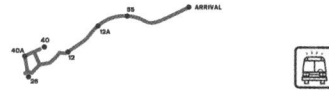

1 ....

2 ....

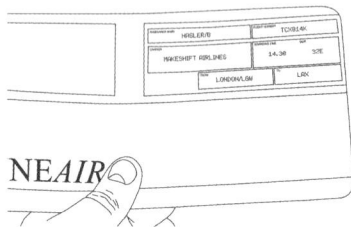

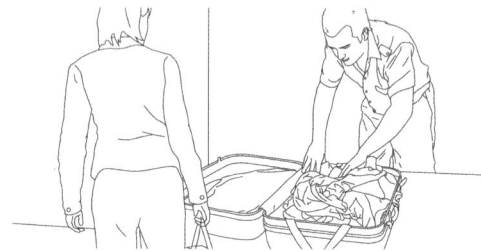

3 ....

4 ....

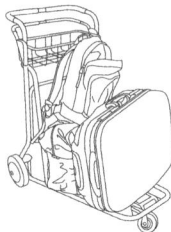

5 ....

6 ....

7 ....

8 ....

(b) Put the prepositions in the box in the correct places.

| at | on | in | at | off | in | to | at |

1 Hurry up and get .... the car – we're late!

2 I'm going to visit my cousins in Australia – I'm going to arrive .... the airport in the evening.

3 It was very cold when I arrived .... New York.

4 It took over 20 minutes for everyone to get .... the plane.

5 The plane should arrive .... six o'clock, but it's delayed.

6 We arrived .... the airport too late – we missed the plane!

7 According to the travel agent, we'll travel .... Madrid from Barcelona on Sunday.

8 The plane for Prague takes .... at 5.30.

4 Culture in mind

a Read the text. Choose the most suitable summary (1–7) for each paragraph (A–F). The first one is done for you. There is one summary you won't use.

1 Saying goodbye ☐

2 Saved from the sea ☐

3 A 'first' for women [A]

4 Love of the sea ☐

5 No giving up ☐

6 Big trouble with a storm ☐

7 Previous achievements ☐

b Read the questions. (Circle) the correct answers, a, b, c or d.

1 Where is Tori Murden McClure from?

a Alaska   b the Canary Islands
c the USA   d Kenya

2 Which of the following activities has Tori McClure *not* done?

a rowing   b snowboarding   c skiing
d mountain climbing

3 How many times did her boat turn over in the 1998 journey?

a five   b six   c ten   d eleven

4 Why couldn't they get her boat out of the sea?

a The sea was too rough.
b The boat was badly damaged.
c The boat was near Portugal.
d The boat had capsized.

5 Why did she not break the Transatlantic rowing record?

a She had problems with her shoulder.
b She ran into a hurricane.
c She had to stop and repair her boat.
d Her boat turned over.

Tori Murden McClure: solo rower

A In 1999, 36-year-old Tori Murden McClure became the first woman to row solo across the Atlantic Ocean, from the Canary Islands to the Caribbean. The journey of just over 5,300 kilometres took the American 81 days. Her boat, The American Pearl, was only 35 metres long.

B McClure is a real adventurer. She has been on many mountaineering expeditions, including climbs in Alaska, Kenya and Antarctica. She was also the youngest person in a team that skied 1,200 kilometres across Antarctica to the South Pole in 1989, and became one of only two women ever to travel to the Pole overland.

C The journey across the Atlantic was her third attempt. The first time she failed because of illness, and during her second attempt, in 1998, she nearly died. She had rowed nearly 5,000 kilometres when her boat was hit by Hurricane Danielle. McClure was suddenly in the middle of 80 kph winds, and surrounded by waves that were 20 metres high.

D Her little boat turned over five times. McClure was sure that she was going to die – she took the video recorder that she had brought with her and recorded a farewell message to her family and friends. The hurricane continued into the night, and The American Pearl turned over five more times.

E McClure was determined not to send a signal asking to be rescued – she didn't want other people to risk their lives, too. But after the eleventh capsizing of her boat, she finally sent it and a large ship came and found her. However, they couldn't get her boat out of the rough sea – it was found months later near the coast of Portugal.

F Tori McClure had concussion and a dislocated shoulder when she got home. Many people might have given up after an experience such as this, but one year later, McClure was back in her repaired boat and trying again. This time she was successful - and although she again met a hurricane on the journey, which stopped her from breaking the record for the fastest Transatlantic rowing crossing, she only overturned once!

5 Vocabulary

Movement

Use one of the phrasal verbs in the box (in the correct form) to complete each sentence.

go back   take off   head for   touch down

1 We need to get to the airport soon – our plane _____ at eight o'clock.

2 I think we're lost! Perhaps we should try to _____ the way we came.

3 He got in his car and _____ London.

4 The spacecraft _____ on the planet Mars yesterday morning.

Skills in mind

6 Read

a Read the text. Put these six phrases/sentences into the correct spaces (A–F).

1 but a new one began
2 Gagarin died in a plane crash in 1968
3 it was a journey that put his name into the list of history's greatest travellers
4 it was the trip from the bus to the spacecraft that took the most courage
5 for example, Vostok's re-entry into the Earth's atmosphere was faster than it should have been
6 Gagarin was just a passenger and had no control at all over the spacecraft

Yuri Gagarin
into the unknown

On April 12 1961, a 27-year-old Russian pilot named Yuri Gagarin became the first person to travel in space. His spacecraft Vostok (which means 'East' in Russian) was operated completely by the people on the ground – ^A _____ .

It was not a long trip. Gagarin returned to Earth after travelling at 27,400 kilometres per hour for only 108 minutes, and Vostok did not even make a complete orbit of the Earth – it landed a few kilometres from where it was launched. It was also Gagarin's one and only journey in space; however, ^B _____ _____ .

Gagarin became a hero in the USSR. He was given awards and went on parades in many countries around the world. However, few Soviet citizens, or anyone else, knew all the details of Gagarin's flight, which were kept secret at the time. In fact, there were many technical problems on the journey – ^C _____ _____ .

For many years, the United States and the then Soviet Union had been racing to see which country could put a man into space first. Gagarin's journey ended that race, ^D _____ _____ – to see who could be first to land on the moon, a race which the Americans won eight years later when Armstrong and Aldrin touched down on the moon's surface.

^E _____ . Flying on a cloudy day, Gagarin thought he was several hundred metres high when his fighter plane hit the ground – he died immediately.

People will always remember Gagarin for his famous trip into space in 1961. But one space historian said that ^F _____ _____ . 'That was on his own legs. Gagarin chose to put himself into the unknown.

b Read the text again. Mark the statements *T* (true), *F* (false) or *N* (not enough information).

1 Gagarin was a military pilot. ☐
2 He was in space for over two hours. ☐
3 He never went into space again. ☐
4 Gagarin nearly died when Vostok came back into the Earth's atmosphere. ☐
5 Armstrong and Aldrin landed on the moon in 1969. ☐
6 Gagarin died when his plane exploded in flight. ☐

Reading tip

Putting phrases/sentences into a text

- Always read the complete text first.

- Remember that some phrases will be easier to put back than others – do the easy ones first.

- Read very carefully the sentence before each gap and make sure you understand it – then look for a phrase which has a meaning connection. For example, the sentence before gap C says that 'there were technical problems on the journey' – so look for a phrase which talks about difficulties with the journey.

Unit check

1 Fill in the spaces

Complete the text with the words in the box.

~~at~~   customs   flight   got into   hero   took off   solo   touched down   welcome   won

On May 20 1927, [1] _____ at _____ 7.52 a.m., Charles Lindbergh [2] _____ his plane 'The Spirit of St Louis'.
He [3] _____ from Long Island, USA, and set off towards Europe to become the first man to fly
[4] _____ across the Atlantic Ocean. His [5] _____ took 33 hours. When he [6] _____
in Paris, 100,000 people were waiting for him – and he didn't have to go through [7] _____ !
Lindbergh, aged 25, [8] _____ a prize of $25,000 – a very large amount of money at that time.
He became an instant American [9] _____ . When he got back to New York, the city gave him an
enormous [10] _____ – the biggest ticker-tape parade in the city's history.

`9`

2 Choose the correct answers

Circle the correct answers, a, b or c.

1 Hurry up or we'll _____ the plane!
  a (miss) b catch c take
2 The traffic's terrible – I think _____ really late!
  a I will be b I'm being c I'm going to be
3 Do you think we can all get _____ such a small car?
  a on b in c at
4 Sorry I'm late. I got _____ the wrong bus.
  a at b in c on
5 You should check _____ an hour before the flight.
  a in b out c off

6 I met an old friend in the _____ lounge.
  a leaving b left c departure
7 My mother went on a business _____ to Japan last month.
  a trip b journey c travel
8 Sue's late, but I'm sure _____ soon.
  a she'll arrive b she's arriving c she arrives
9 Hello! Welcome to London! Did you have a good _____ ?
  a travel b journey c tour

`8`

3 Correct the mistakes

In each sentence there is a mistake with the present continuous, *going to* or *will*. Underline the mistakes and write the correct sentence.

1 My sister <u>are</u> going to help me.   *My sister is going to help me.* _____
2 I'll to do my homework tonight. _____
3 I seeing the doctor tomorrow morning. _____
4 I think it's going snow this afternoon. _____
5 My parents and I am going to fly to Paris tomorrow. _____
6 The traffic's very bad – we not will arrive on time. _____
7 What are you go to study at university? _____
8 What time do you leaving tomorrow morning? _____
9 We having a party on Friday – do you want to come? _____

`8`

How did you do?

Total: `25`

| 😊 | Very good 20 – 25 | 😐 | OK 14 – 19 | 🙁 | Review Unit 5 again 0 – 13 |

⑥ Live forever!

① Grammar
Future predictions

ⓐ Complete the sentences with the correct form of *(not) be likely to*.

1 'It's nice, but it *'s likely to* be really expensive.'

2 'Please write it down, because I _____ forget.'

3 'You _____ fail the exam.'

4 'He _____ play again for about six months.'

5 'I _____ pass, am I?'

6 'Perhaps we shouldn't play here – we _____ break something.'

ⓑ Complete the sentences. Use the information in the chart.

100%	will	
75%	will probably	be likely to
50%	might	might not
25%	probably won't	not be likely to
0%	won't	

1 It / rain at the weekend. (75% + *will*)
   It will probably rain at the weekend.

2 My parents / be unhappy with my results. (100%)

3 My brother / arrive late tomorrow. (75% + *likely*)

4 The match on Saturday / be very good. (0%)

5 I / go to the cinema this evening. (50%)

6 I / pass next week's test. (75% + *likely*)

7 They / be at home tomorrow. (25% + *not likely*)

8 There / be much to eat at the party. (25% + *won't*)

9 We / visit our grandparents next weekend. (50% + *not*)

ⓒ Rewrite the sentences. Use the words in brackets.

1 The chances of my father buying me a computer are small. **(likely)**
   My father isn't likely to buy me a computer.

2 It's possible that I will pass the exams. **(might)**

3 It's possible that he won't arrive on time. **(might not)**

4 I'm almost sure that I'll be late. **(probably)**

5 There is a small chance my mother will lend me some money. **(not likely)**

6 I don't think that my sister will buy that car. **(probably won't)**

7 It's very possible that they will be at the party. **(likely)**

2 Grammar

First conditional, *if* and *unless*

a Complete the sentences with the present simple form of the verbs, or *will/won't*.

1 I *will lend* (lend) you the money if you *promise* (promise) to give it back tomorrow.
2 If she _____ (phone) me tonight, I _____ (ask) her to go out with me.
3 The door _____ (not open) unless you _____ (push) it hard.
4 Unless we _____ (leave) now, we _____ (be) late for school.
5 If he _____ (not be) careful, he _____ (hurt) himself.
6 I _____ (not come) if you _____ (not want) me to.
7 Unless you _____ (stop) talking, the teacher _____ (get) angry with you.
8 The dog _____ (not bite) you if you _____ (leave) it alone.

b Make the sentences.

1 you / have an accident / unless / you go more slowly
You'll have an accident unless you go more slowly.

2 If / John / invite me to the party, / I / go
_____

3 I / beat Sally / unless / I / play badly
_____

4 I / be very upset / if / he / lose my camera
_____

5 Unless / you / go now, / the shops / be closed
_____

6 If / my friend / come round, / we / play computer games
_____

3 Grammar

Time conjunctions: *if / unless / when / until / as soon as*

a Circle the correct words.

1 I'll tell you *until / as soon as* I know.
2 Mary isn't here yet so let's wait *until / when* she arrives.
3 I'm going to buy a new computer *when / unless* I have enough money.
4 You won't pass the exams *if / unless* you study more.
5 We'll go out *as soon as / unless* the weather gets better.
6 I'll stay at home *as soon as / until* it stops raining.
7 *When / Unless* we move house, I'll have my own bedroom.
8 *If / Until* I fail my driving test, I'll take it again.

b Complete each space. Use *if, unless, until* or *as soon as*.

1 She's coming home at 6.00. I'll talk to her _____ she arrives.
2 _____ we hurry up, we'll be late for the film!
3 Dad's picking us up in the car, so we'll have to wait _____ he gets here.
4 What will you do _____ you don't pass your exams?
5 Can you do me a favour? Look after my cat _____ I get back from holiday, please.
6 I can't buy it _____ my parents lend me some money.
7 I can't talk now, I'm watching a football match – but I'll ring you _____ it finishes, OK?
8 _____ the cinema's full, don't worry – we can come back home and watch a video.

4 Vocabulary

Verbs with prepositions

(a) Find five words in the grid to complete the phrases.

G	A	R	G	E	T	T	I	N	G
R	R	E	O	V	T	H	N	E	R
O	G	A	R	R	H	I	R	A	E
W	O	R	R	Y	I	N	G	R	V
O	I	N	A	N	N	K	O	N	I
R	V	I	S	I	K	O	I	I	S
I	W	N	K	G	I	N	N	G	I
A	R	G	U	I	N	G	G	T	N
N	Y	R	R	I	G	O	I	R	G
G	E	T	T	I	N	G	S	W	

Common causes of stress:

1 _____ with people
2 _____ about your problems
3 _____ for exams
4 _____ about what to wear
5 _____ ready for school

(b) Complete the sentences with the expressions in Exercise 4a.

1 I hate _____ !
   I almost always forget a book or something.

2 My brother's going to a party tonight, and he's
   spent hours _____ .

3 I think _____ is
   pointless! Either you've learned the things
   already, or you haven't!

4 Don't sit _____
   – go and do something about them!

5 He's a really unpleasant guy – he's always
   _____ and fighting.

(c) Complete the sentences with the correct
   prepositions.

1 I'm a bit worried _____ my sister.

2 My parents are thinking _____ moving
   to another town.

3 School ends next week, so I'm getting ready
   _____ the summer holidays.

4 Which exam are you revising _____ ?

5 Why are you always arguing _____ your
   parents?

6 What are you waiting _____ ?

5 Pronunciation

Strong and weak forms of prepositions

🔊 Listen and repeat. Pay particular
attention to the underlined words.

1 I'm looking <u>for</u> my books.
2 What are you waiting <u>for</u>?
3 Sorry – I don't want to talk <u>to</u> you.
4 Who are you writing <u>to</u>?
5 Are you looking <u>at</u> me?
6 Who are you looking <u>at</u>?

6 Everyday English

a Put the words into the correct order to make the phrases.

1 is fact the ....

2 you me between and ....

3 mean you know I what ....

4 not or it believe ....

b Use one of the phrases above to complete each space in the dialogue.

Steve: Hey, Andy. You look really fed up. What's the matter?

Andy: Hmm. Well, yes, I am a bit – but I don't really want to talk about it.

Steve: Oh come on, Andy – you can tell me. What is it?

Andy: OK, I'll tell you – but this is

¹ .... , OK?

Steve: Sure. I won't tell anyone.

Andy: Well, I asked Jane to go out with me tomorrow – I was sure she'd say No, but

² .... ,

she said Yes!

Steve: Great! So, what's the problem?

Andy: Well,

³ .... , I just don't know where I'm going to take her.

Steve: Yeah, ⁴ .... – I always feel that way, the first time I take a girl out. Look, why don't you take her to that new club in George Street?

Andy: Yeah, that's a good idea – maybe I'll do that. But is it expensive?

7 Study help

Learning and recording words in context

- It's very important to record words that you learn in a context – in other words, don't record them as words on their own.

- For example: if you learn the verb 'worry', you <u>could</u> record it as one word and then write a translation, e.g. 'worry = se preocupar'.

- But in order to <u>use</u> the word 'worry', you need to know and remember words that go with it – e.g. the preposition 'about'. So it's much better to write a sentence or phrase that uses the other words too, e.g. 'She never seems to worry about anything'. (You can add a translation if you think it's important and useful.)

- It's also a good idea to record <u>your own</u> sentences/phrases, about things which are true for you – this makes new language much more memorable.

Write sentences/phrases in your notebook (or here) which will help you remember and use these words from the unit:

argue ....

get ready ....

unless ....

as soon as ....

likely ....

Skills in mind

8 Write

a Read this advertisement in a newspaper. The advertisement requests information about four different things. What are they?

☼ SUMMER CAMPS UK ☼

Wanted: young people to work on a holiday camp for 10–13-year-old children in the UK for a period of three months. Various locations in the country. The work includes organising entertainment for the children and general cleaning duties.

If you are interested in this position, write and tell us:

- ☼ why you think you are suitable for the post
- ☼ about your level of English (exams you have passed / hope to pass in the future)
- ☼ what you think you will gain from working with younger children
- ☼ what you think you will gain or learn from being in the UK for three months.

Write to PO Box 788, Cheltenham, UK before April 30 this year

---

b A young man called André wrote a letter to apply for one of the jobs. Read his letter and say which of the four requests for information in the advertisement he <u>doesn't</u> respond to.

Dear Sir or Madam

I am writing to apply for a summer camp job in the UK.

I am an independent and reliable person. [1] <u>Unless I get one of the jobs</u>, I will work hard and I am sure that I will be a good employee.

I think that you need patience and a good sense of humour to work with younger children. I believe I have these qualities, but I also think that [2] <u>they are likely improve</u> through this work. I think I will also learn how to deal with difficult children, and to provide discipline when it is needed.

It has always been my dream to visit Britain. I believe that my English will improve, and I am sure that I [3] <u>will to learn</u> a lot of things about a different and foreign culture.

[4] <u>Thank you for consider</u> my application. I look forward to your reply.

Yours faithfully

André Le Bendit

c Each of the <u>underlined</u> phrases 1–4 contains a language mistake. Correct each one.

d Imagine that you want to apply for one of the summer camp jobs. Write your letter in about 120–180 words. (Don't count the opening and your name.)

Writing tip

Writing a letter for an exam

When you write a letter, especially for a test or an examination, remember that you should always:

- Read the task carefully and do exactly what it asks you to do. In this example, you need to read the advertisement carefully and make sure that you provide <u>all</u> the information that the advertisement asks for. If you miss out important information, you will lose a lot of marks.

- Check your own writing carefully when you have finished. Check for grammar mistakes and for any spelling mistakes. In exams especially, it is easy to make small mistakes under pressure. Give yourself time at the end to check.

- Check your text, if there is a word limit, to make sure that you have used about the required number of words. If you don't write enough words, you will lose marks. If you write far too many, the examiner won't mark much beyond the word limit.

Unit check

1 Fill in the spaces

Complete the text with the words in the box.

| until | If | unless | likely | might | probably | for | about | ~~when~~ | with |

I'm not very sure what to do ¹ ___*when*___ I leave school. ² _____ I do well in my exams, I ³ _____ go to university, but I ⁴ _____ won't get good enough grades – I haven't revised ⁵ _____ the exams very much at all. So I think that perhaps I'll get a job, save some money and then travel a bit, ⁶ _____ I haven't got any money left. When I told my parents about that, they weren't very happy and they argued ⁷ _____ me for a long time. They said they were worried ⁸ _____ me, and they didn't want me to go. And I don't think they're ⁹ _____ to change their minds. So, ¹⁰ _____ I can think of something else, I still won't know what to do when I leave school!

> 9

2 Choose the correct answers

(Circle) the correct answers, a, b or c.

1 _____ the weather's nice this weekend, we can have a picnic.
   a (If) b When c As soon as

2 Why do you always argue _____ me?
   a to b at c with

3 I can't come out tonight – I'm revising _____ my exams.
   a for b about c to

4 I don't want to leave – I want to stay _____ the film finishes.
   a until b if c when

5 I'll phone you as soon as I _____ anything.
   a am hearing b will hear c hear

6 I can't stand her – she only ever thinks _____ herself.
   a for b about c with

7 They won't know _____ you don't tell them.
   a unless b when c if

8 Mike's upstairs – he's _____ ready for tonight's party.
   a going b getting c being

9 You won't pass the test _____ you study hard.
   a as soon as b when c unless

> 8

3 Correct the mistakes

In each sentence there is a mistake with making predictions or with the first conditional. <u>Underline</u> the mistakes and write the correct sentence.

1 If I <u>will play</u> squash tomorrow, I'll win. *If I play squash tomorrow, I'll win.*

2 He's likely be late. _____

3 The teacher not might like it. _____

4 I'll tell you the results as soon I know them. _____

5 I'll tell them when they will arrive. _____

6 He not will be happy when he finds out. _____

7 The test is likely to not be very difficult. _____

8 I've got to stay here unless five o'clock tonight. _____

9 Unless they don't invite me to the party, I won't go. _____

> 8

How did you do?

Total: [25]

| ☺ | Very good 20 – 25 | ☺ | OK 14 – 19 | ☹ | Review Unit 6 again 0 – 13 |

7 Campaigning for survival

1 Grammar

Present passive and past passive review

a Circle the correct answers, a, b, c or d.

1 Squash is a popular sport that _____ indoors.
   a plays   b is played   c played   d was played

2 President John Kennedy _____ in Dallas in November 1963.
   a kills   b is killed   c killed   d was killed

3 Many Japanese people _____ sushi and sashimi.
   a eat   b are eaten   c ate   d were eaten

4 Many animals _____ for scientific experiments in the past.
   a use   b are used   c used   d were used

5 Spanish _____ by a lot of people in the USA.
   a speaks   b is spoken   c spoke   d was spoken

6 Honda is a company that _____ cars.
   a makes   b is made   c made   d was made

b Write sentences using the present simple or past simple passive.

1 The World Trade Center / destroy / on 11 September 2001
   The World Trade Center was destroyed on 11 September 2001.

2 A language called Hindi / speak / in many parts of India _____

3 The 2004 Olympic Games / hold / in Athens _____

4 Boeing 747 planes / call / Jumbos _____

5 Most American films / make / in Hollywood _____

6 The 2002 football World Cup / win / by Brazil _____

7 John Lennon / kill / in December 1980 _____

8 The *Titanic* / sink / by an iceberg _____

9 Gorillas / find / in forests in Africa _____

10 Buildings / design / by architects _____

2 Grammar

Causative *have* (*have something done*)

a Look at the signs. Write sentences about what you can have done at each place.

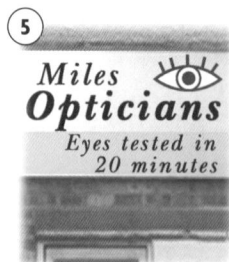

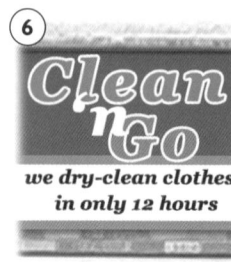

1 Pizza Home — We deliver pizzas FAST!

2 Photo EXPRESS — Bring your film here. We develop in 30 mins

3 Rings & Things — We can pierce your ears in no time at all!

4 Hard and Soft — Let us repair your computer

5 Miles Opticians — Eyes tested in 20 minutes

6 Clean n Go — we dry-clean clothes in only 12 hours

1 You can *have your pizza delivered.*

2 You can have your _____

3 You can _____

4 You _____

5 You _____

6 _____

b 🔊 Look at the pictures and write the sentences. Choose words from the box. Then listen and check.

photograph	~~test~~
computer	repair
car	take
~~eyes~~	cut
hair	build
garage	deliver

1 She *'s having her eyes tested.*

2 They _____ .

3 He _____ .

4 She _____ .

5 He _____ .

6 They _____ .

3 Pronunciation
have something done

a 🔊 Listen again to the sentences in Exercise 2b. Mark the stressed words.

b 🔊 Listen again and repeat the sentences.

4 Vocabulary
make and *do*

a Complete the puzzle. What is the mystery word?

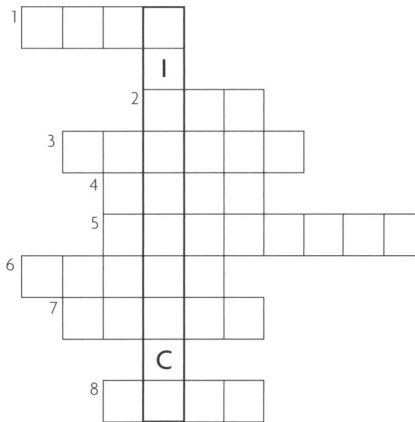

1 Eat fruit! It'll do you a lot of _____ .

2 It's not nice to make _____ of other people.

3 You can do it if you make an _____ .

4 I did my _____ not to laugh at her.

5 I'm working hard, but I'm not making much _____ .

6 He made a lot of _____ when he sold his flat.

7 Why do people smoke? It doesn't make _____ to me!

8 I dropped some paint on the floor – it made a real _____ .

b Complete the sentences with the correct form of *make* or *do*.

1 Don't just sit there! ___*Do*___ something!

2 I took the medicine the doctor gave me and it _____ me a lot of good.

3 I've read this page three times – and it still _____ (not) sense to me!

4 I've got a faster computer now, and it _____ a big difference.

5 Yesterday's exam was hard! But I _____ my best.

6 I had to take the desk out of my bedroom to _____ room for my new stereo system!

7 Well done, Helen. You _____ a lot of progress since last year!

8 I'm going to get a job and _____ some money.

5 Grammar

Present perfect passive

(a) Complete the sentences with the words from the box.

> have been killed   has been made
> have been sold   have been made
> haven't been invited   has been built

1   A new library _____ in our town.

2   Their new CD only came out last week, but
    thousands of copies _____
    already!

3   There's been an earthquake in our country, and a lot
    of people _____ .

4   Many animals _____ extinct in the
    last twenty years.

5   They're having a party tomorrow evening – but we
    _____ !

6   A big effort _____ recently to
    keep the town clean.

(b) What has happened in each picture? Complete the
sentences with the present perfect passive form of
the verbs.

1   The woman _____ . (rob)

2   Three houses _____ . (knock down)

3   Their pizzas _____ (not deliver) yet.

4   The bank robbers _____ . (catch)

5   That car _____ (not clean) for weeks!

6   The fire _____ . (put out)

6 Grammar

Future passive

(a) Look at the poster. What will be done if
they are elected? Complete the sentences.

> # VOTE FOR US!
> *We will ...*
> * build new schools!
> * protect trees and parks!
> * NOT increase taxes!
> * give food to poor families!
> * put more policemen on the streets!
> * NOT close hospitals!
> * help new companies!
> * reduce pollution!

1   New schools
    will be built _____ .

2   Trees and parks
    _____ .

3   Taxes _____ .

4   Food _____
    to poor families.

5   More policemen
    _____ on the
    streets.

6   Hospitals _____ .

7   New companies
    _____ .

8   Pollution _____ .

(b) Complete the sentences/questions. Use the
future passive form of the verbs.

1   A new swimming pool _____
    (build) in our town next year.

2   It _____ (not finish) until next
    October.

3   _____ the water
    _____ (heat) ?

4   All the swimmers _____
    (supervise) by lifeguards.

5   Children under ten _____
    (not allow) to swim without an adult.

6   _____ people who can't
    swim _____ (give) lessons?

7 Fiction in mind

a Here is another extract from *But Was it Murder?* Read the extract quickly and find out:

- who Bowen is talking to
- how many sets of fingerprints were found

CHAPTER 15 Uncovering lies

'Sorry, sir,' said Bowen. 'But I thought you'd want to hear this as soon as possible. It seems that Forley had a cleaning lady, a Mrs Brook. She went to his house this morning, and got angry when they wouldn't let her in. Mondays and Thursdays were the days she worked for him. And she worked for the Crowthers on Wednesdays.

'Anyway, she's given us some very interesting information. It seems that Forley went to see Catherine Crowther on Wednesday afternoon, when Ronald was out.'

'That *is* interesting,' said Eliot. 'Mrs Crowther told us she hadn't [1] .... him for a week. What did Mrs Brook say about the visit?'

'Apparently, Forley was there for about an hour,' Bowen replied. 'The sitting room door was closed, so she couldn't hear anything. But when they came out, Mrs Crowther was as white as a sheet, and Forley looked very uncomfortable.'

'I [2] .... what Catherine Crowther will have to say about that,' said Eliot.

'But that's not all, sir,' continued Bowen. 'Mrs Brook said that Crowther had an old gun. Apparently, it [3] .... belonged to his father. She came into the room once when he was cleaning it. He quickly put it back into a drawer in his desk, but not before she had seen it. She said she could never go into the sitting room again without wondering if it was still there.'

'He kept it in a desk?' said Eliot. 'That was stupid. And I don't suppose he had a licence for it. Well, that gives us [4] .... to think about. What about the fingerprints? Have you had any luck with them?'

'Well, sir,' said Bowen. 'There were four sets of fresh fingerprints found in the house besides Forley's.'

'So, all we have to do is find out whose fingerprints they are. Our suspects are the Crowthers, the Wilvers, Amanda Grant and Mrs Brook. Can we be sure about what any of them were doing on Friday afternoon?'

'Well we know Mrs Brook spent the day with her sister. And Wilver was in the surgery from twelve forty-five to six o'clock,' said Bowen. 'He had two meetings, and then he saw patients. He didn't have a free moment. And his wife [5] .... lunch with a friend in Greenwich. She left at three-fifteen to pick up her son from school.'

'What about the other three?' asked Eliot.

'We haven't been able to check their [6] .... ,' said Bowen. 'Catherine Crowther was alone at home. Ronald was out walking, but he doesn't remember seeing anybody. And Amanda Grant went straight to her house when she got back.

'But there's something else, sir,' he continued. 'I looked at a few more pages of Forley's diary while I was waiting at the surgery, and I found something very [7] .... It seems Alex Forley wasn't the golden boy everybody thinks he was. He was having a secret love affair.'

b Read the extract again. Circle the correct answers, a, b, c or d to complete each space (1–7).

1 a had	b seen	c seeing	d was
2 a ask	b think	c feel	d wonder
3 a was	b been	c is	d had
4 a something	b nothing	c anything	d everything
5 a has	b been having	c had had	d was having
6 a reasons	b stories	c lies	d truth
7 a interesting	b interested	c mystery	d wrong

c Answer the questions.

1 What was Mrs Brook's job?

....

2 Who did Forley see on Wednesday afternoon?

....

3 Where did Crowther keep his gun?

....

4 Which of the suspects had the best excuse?

....

d Who do you think killed Mr Forley? Why?

Skills in mind

8 Listen

🔊 Listen to five short recordings. For each one, ⟨circle⟩ the correct answer, a, b or c.

1 Listen to a teacher who is talking to a group of students about a bus. What time will the bus leave?

    a 8.15
    b 8.30
    c 8.50

2 Listen to a teacher talking to a girl, Sally, about her results. What does the Maths teacher think about Sally's results?

    a She's very happy with Sally's progress.
    b She thinks that Sally could make more progress.
    c She's very angry that Sally hasn't made progress.

3 Mike is talking to Andy. What is different about Andy?

    a He's had his hair cut.
    b He's had his arm tattooed.
    c He's had his ear pierced.

4 A news announcer is talking about an earthquake. How many people have been killed?

    a About four thousand.
    b About four hundred.
    c About fourteen thousand.

5 Listen to a phone conversation – a woman is ordering a pizza. How much will she have to pay for the pizza?

    a £6.25 plus 30p for delivery.
    b £6.25 if she wants the pizza in the next 30 minutes.
    c Nothing if the pizza is not delivered within 30 minutes.

Listening tip

How to answer multiple choice questions

- Read all the choices carefully and make sure you understand them. What do you have to listen for? For example, in number one you have to listen for a time.

- Remember that you will need to listen to the whole section before you choose your answer. Never write down the first thing you hear. For example, in number 1, the woman tells the students to be back at the bus at 8.15, but that isn't when the bus will leave. She then goes on to say it will leave 'at half past'. So, what time does the bus leave?

- Remember that you can usually hear the recording twice. Use the second listening either to check your answer, or to help you think about the correct answer.

Unit check

1 Fill in the spaces

Complete the text with the words in the box.

were   was   have   had   ~~went~~   developed   made   made   taken   effort

Last year I needed a new passport, so I ¹ _____went_____ to a photo shop in town and had my photograph
² _____ , but when I went back two days later to collect the photo, I looked at it and thought it
³ _____ awful! The colour was strange, and I was sure it hadn't been ⁴ _____ properly, so
I complained to the man in the shop. I said: 'You've ⁵ _____ a mess of this!', but he ⁶ _____
fun of me. So I talked to the manager, who asked me if I wanted to ⁷ _____ my photo taken again.
I wasn't very happy, but I said OK, sat down and made a big ⁸ _____ to smile. This time I
⁹ _____ three photos taken, but when I saw them they ¹⁰ _____ worse than the first one
because I looked so angry!

`9`

2 Choose the correct answers

(Circle) the correct answers, a, b or c.

1   Work hard and you'll _____ progress.
    a do   b (make) c have

2   I need to throw some old clothes away, to make
    _____ for the new ones.
    a room   b a mess   c an effort

3   My dad's car broke down, so he had to
    _____ it repaired.
    a have   b do   c make

4   If you pronounce a language well, it makes a big
    _____ for other people.
    a mess   b difference   c progress

5   A prehistoric man _____ last year.
    a was found   b find   c is found

6   She went to the hairdresser's to _____ .
    a cut her hair   b have cut her hair   c have
    her hair cut

7   Eating fruit can do you a lot of _____ .
    a best   b good   c better

8   Since last year, a lot of new roads _____ .
    a have been built   b were built   c have built

9   The government says that next year, taxes
    _____ .
    a will reduce   b will be reduced   c have
    reduced

`8`

3 Correct the mistakes

In each sentence there is a mistake with causative *have* or the passive. Underline the mistakes and
write the correct sentence.

1   BMW cars is made in Germany.   _BMW cars are made in Germany._ _____

2   I'm going to the hairdresser's to cut my hair. _____

3   Pandas found in the forests in China. _____

4   I took my car to the garage and had repaired it. _____

5   You can't buy this car because it's be sold already. _____

6   I took my film to a shop and developed it. _____

7   Three cars was stolen in our street last night. _____

8   The new pool won't build until next year. _____

9   Yesterday, two criminals have been arrested. _____

`8`

How did you do?

Total: `25`

| ☺ | Very good 20 – 25 | ☺ | OK 14 – 19 | ☹ | Review Unit 7 again 0 – 13 |

(8) Reality TV

1 Grammar

make / let / be allowed to

(a) Put the words in the correct order.

1 a noise / aren't / to / You / make / allowed
You aren't allowed to make a noise. .

2 travellers / to / the / allowed / enter / weren't / the country
_____ .

3 parents / play outside / let / Our / never / us
_____ .

4 us / The / didn't / leave / early / let / teacher
_____ .

5 mobile / made / switch off / our / They / us / phones
_____ .

6 made / The / were / a / test / children / do / to
_____ .

(b) Look at the signs. Write sentences with *(not) allowed to.*

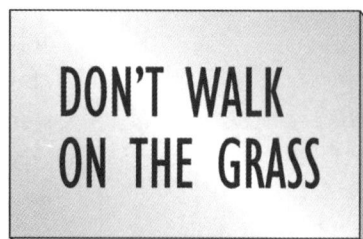

1 *You aren't allowed to cycle / ride your bike here.*

2 _____ .

3 _____ .

4 _____ .

5 _____ .

6 _____

but _____ .

(c) Rewrite the sentences using the words in brackets.

1 We don't have permission to go into that room. **(allowed)**
We aren't allowed to go into that room.

2 The teacher told us to stay longer at school yesterday. **(made)**
The teacher _____ .

3 I don't allow my sister to borrow my things. **(let)**
I _____ .

4 My father didn't give me permission to borrow his car. **(let)**
My father _____ .

5 You can't smoke here. **(allowed)**
You _____ .

6 We had to tidy our rooms last Saturday. **(made)**
We _____ .

2 Vocabulary

Television

(a) Complete the crossword by solving the clues with words from page 53 of the Student's Book.

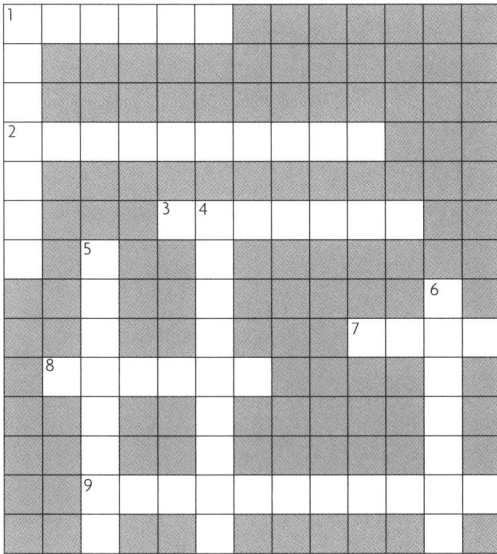

1(→) A group of programmes about the same subject.

1(↓) Comedy programmes about the lives of ordinary people.

2 A person who takes part in a '7'.

3 One part of a 1(↓).

4 The person who presents a programme.

5 People who watch a TV programme in the studio.

6 The number of people who watch a programme is called the viewing _____ .

7 A programme where people answer questions is a _____ show.

8 A person who is watching a TV programme at home (not in the studio).

9 Well-known people on television (or in films).

(b) Complete the sentences with the correct form of the word at the end of each line.

Yesterday evening I watched a ¹ _wonderful_ new quiz show on TV. WONDER

There are four ² _____ , who have to answer really hard CONTEST

questions that the ³ _____ asks them. If they don't know the answer to PRESENT

a question, they are ⁴ _____ to phone home and get some help. And ALLOW

sometimes the ⁵ _____ at home can phone the programme and ask VIEW

questions too. The ⁶ _____ gets a prize of a new car! I think WIN

it's going to be a very ⁷ _____ show. SUCCESS

3 Pronunciation

/aʊ/ allowed

(a) 🔊 Tick (✓) the words which have the sound /aʊ/ in them. Then listen, check and repeat.

1 how ☐
2 know ☐
3 now ☐
4 mouse ☐
5 loud ☐
6 shout ☐
7 slow ☐
8 house ☐
9 found ☐
10 snow ☐

(b) 🔊 Listen and repeat.

1 How do you know which house it is?

2 I found a mouse in the snow.

3 We heard a loud shout.

4 There was a mouse running loudly round the house.

4 Grammar

Modal verbs of obligation, prohibition and permission

(a) Complete the sentences with the words in the box.

have to go   mustn't go   can't bring
don't have to stay   can stay   must bring

1 'OK, tomorrow afternoon is sports, so you _____ your sports clothes, OK?'

2 'Great! My dad says I _____ out as late as I want to.'

3 'Sorry, I'm really late for my meeting. I _____ now.'

4 'Are you bored? Well, look – you _____ here if you don't want to.'

5 'Hey, Alex, that's the girls' toilet, you _____ in there!'

6 'Sorry, you _____ your dog into the library. No animals are allowed in here.'

b Look at the pictures. What are the people saying? Complete the sentences.

1 'We _can't_ leave through here.'

2 'You _____ feed the animals!'

3 'You _____ open it now if you want.'

4 'We _____ show something to prove we're 18.'

5 'I _____ clear up this mess!'

6 'Great! I _____ wear a suit and tie!'

5 Vocabulary
Extreme adjectives

a Complete the sentences with the words in the box.

> fantastic enormous boiling
> exhausted ~~tiny~~ starving
> freezing

1 A: Look at that insect – it's really small!
  B: Small? It's _tiny_ !

2 A: Was it hot in Australia?
  B: Yes it was! In fact, it was _____ !

3 A: This is a good song.
  B: Yes, it's _____ !

4 A: Is it cold outside?
  B: It's _____ !

5 A: Is her new flat big?
  B: It certainly is. In fact, it's _____ !

6 A: Are you hungry?
  B: I'm _____ !

7 A: I think Alex is tired.
  B: Tired? He's _____ !

b Complete the sentences with *very*, *really* or *absolutely*. There are usually two possibilities.

1 I thought the film was _really_ / _absolutely_ fantastic!

2 A: What was your holiday like?
  B: Well, the weather was _____ / _____ nice but the hotel was _____ / _____ awful!

3 I got _____ / _____ bad marks for Geography, but my Maths marks were _____ / _____ brilliant!

4 I wasn't _____ / _____ hungry before, but now I'm _____ / _____ starving!

5 A: The water's _____ / _____ cold.
  B: It isn't cold, it's _____ / _____ freezing!

6 Jean's got _____ / _____ strange green hair!

6 Vocabulary
Collocations with *on*

Complete the sentences with *on* and words from the box.

> holiday offer the phone strike time TV

1 There's never anything very good _____ in the morning!

2 Unless the plane arrives _____ , we'll miss the next flight.

3 My sister spends hours _____ talking to her boyfriend.

4 All the teachers went _____ yesterday for better pay.

5 We went to Greece _____ , and we had a great time!

6 They've got some great things _____ in the CD shop.

7 Culture in mind

a) Read the text about this song. Some of the lines of the text have an extra, unnecessary word. Write the word at the end of the line. If the line is correct, put a tick (✓).

Somebody's Watching Me by Rockwell

The song *Somebody's Watching Me* ~~it~~ was recorded by a singer called	1	*it*
Rockwell. Rockwell was in fact a man called Kennedy Gordy, who was	2	✓
the son of Berry Gordy, the man who he started Motown records.	3	
Gordy changed his the name because he wanted to make records, but he	4	
also did wanted to be recognised for his talent. He signed with Motown	5	
as a solo artist without his father's knowledge, and took his name from an	6	
American artist. Rockwell's sister, Hazel, was married to the Jermaine Jackson,	7	
Michael Jackson's brother, and that's why Rockwell was able to can get Michael	8	
and Jermaine to sing with on the recording. The song was a big hit and went	9	
to number 2 in the charts in 1984. Rockwell then revealed his true identity.	10	
But he didn't have any more success and his next album didn't sell well not at all.	11	

b) Read the text again. Mark the statements *T* (true), *F* (false) or *N* (information not given).

1 Rockwell's real name was Berry Gordy. ☐

2 Motown records started in Detroit, USA. ☐

3 Berry Gordy knew that his son had signed with Motown. ☐

4 Jermaine Jackson was Rockwell's brother-in-law. ☐

5 *Somebody's Watching Me* was a successful single. ☐

6 Rockwell's next album sold less than ten thousand copies. ☐

c) 🔊 Listen to Dave telling a friend about the video for *Somebody's Watching Me*. Put the pictures in the correct order. Write numbers 1–6 in the boxes.

d) Here are three lines from the song. Which pictures are they related to?

1 But maybe showers remind me of *Psycho* too much.

2 Well, can the people on TV see me or am I just paranoid?

3 Well, is the mailman watching me?

Skills in mind

8 Write

(a) Paul and Sandra had to write articles for their school magazine. Do not write anything yet, but read what they had to do:

Write an article about your favourite television programme. Write about:

- the kind of programme it is, and how often it is on TV
- who the people in the programme are
- what the programme is about
- what you especially like in the programme and why
- who you would recommend it to

Write between 120 and 150 words.

(b) Read Paul and Sandra's answers. Complete the sentences with the words from the box.

been going   very believable   no matter   on the market   a good reason

My favourite programme is *Top Gear*. It's a programme about cars, and I love it because I'm a car freak but also because the presenters are really funny, especially Jeremy Clarkson. They look at new cars that are [1] _____ , and sometimes they're really critical (for example, once Jeremy Clarkson said a car was very cheap, and there was [2] _____ – it was awful!).

There are three presenters – the other two are Richard Hammond and James May. It's on once a week, usually at about 8.00 in the evening.

(Paul – 115 words)

My favourite programme is a soap opera on BBC called *EastEnders*. It's on twice a week, on Tuesday and Thursday evenings, for half an hour each time. It's a story about the lives of people who live in a place called Albert Square, in the east of London. It started in 1985, so the programme's [3] _____ for about twenty years now!

The reason why I like EastEnders is that the characters are really interesting and you get into their lives. There's a good range of characters, and real things happen to them – illness, divorce, marriage, arguments and so on – so it's [4] _____ . The acting is excellent, too.

I think that anyone who enjoys well-written and well-acted soap operas would love EastEnders. There's something in it for everyone, [5] _____ how old they are or whether they're a boy or a girl.

(Sandra – 145 words)

(c) Which of the two articles do you think is better? Why?

(d) Write an article for your school magazine. Use the same task as Paul and Sandra's.

Unit check

1 Fill in the spaces

Complete the text with the words in the box.

> fun   winner   presenter   contestants   freezing   ~~episodes~~   had   allowed   made   enormous

I'll always remember one of the ¹ ___episodes___ of *Endurance*, the Japanese game show. There were six ² _____ , and they were taken to Holland in the middle of winter. They were ³ _____ to take off almost all their clothes and they ⁴ _____ to stand outside in the ⁵ _____ weather. Then the ⁶ _____ told them to drink as much water as they possibly could. And they did – they all drank ⁷ _____ amounts of water! But that wasn't the competition. When they finished drinking, the presenter told them that they weren't ⁸ _____ to go to the toilet! The ⁹ _____ was the last person to go to the toilet. The presenter made ¹⁰ _____ of them too – it was hilarious!

9

2 Choose the correct answers

Circle the correct answers, a, b or c.

1 The _____ in the studio enjoyed the programme a lot.
   a viewing   b (audience)   c ratings

2 We don't like wearing a uniform, but the school _____ us wear one.
   a makes   b lets   c allowed

3 This soap opera has the highest _____ of any TV programme in history!
   a viewers   b ratings   c contestants

4 The water was very cold – in fact, it was really _____ !
   a starving   b boiling   c freezing

5 It's a holiday today, so we _____ go to school.
   a don't have to   b must   c have to

6 I watched the first six _____ of the series, but then I got bored.
   a ratings   b celebrities   c episodes

7 One day I want to be a _____ in a quiz show – I'm sure I'd win!
   a presenter   b viewer   c contestant

8 A few minutes ago, I was hungry – but now I'm absolutely _____ !
   a tiny   b starving   c exhausted

9 If a pupil does something wrong, he or she is _____ to stay longer after school.
   a let   b allowed   c made

8

3 Correct the mistakes

In each sentence there is a mistake with *make / let / be allowed to* or modal verbs. Underline the mistakes and write the correct sentence.

1 We weren't <u>allowed go</u>.   *We weren't allowed to go.* _____

2 You isn't allowed to come in without asking. _____

3 We wanted to go out, but our parents didn't make us. _____

4 Sorry, madam – you can't to park your car here. _____

5 The teacher let us to leave early yesterday. _____

6 I was made wear a uniform. _____

7 I'm not deaf – you have to shout! _____

8 This a no-smoking area – you can smoke in here. _____

9 We're late – we mustn't hurry up! _____

8

How did you do?

Total: [25]

| ☺ | Very good 20 – 25 | ☺ | OK 14 – 19 | ☹ | Review Unit 8 again 0 – 13 |

(9) Good and evil

1 Grammar

Verbs with gerunds;
verbs with infinitives

(a) Find and (circle): seven verbs that are
followed by a gerund (→←) and seven
verbs that are followed by the infinitive.
(↓↑)

W	E	R	E	N	J	O	Y	E	E
P	T	O	U	X	G	F	L	P	S
R	Q	W	F	I	O	F	O	V	O
O	Z	T	S	E	T	E	D	X	O
M	I	N	D	E	E	R	R	J	H
I	M	A	G	I	N	E	O	L	C
S	U	G	G	E	S	T	F	E	H
E	K	I	L	L	E	E	F	A	O
P	S	E	S	I	T	C	A	R	P
O	A	E	V	I	L	O	S	N	E

(b) Complete the sentences with the
gerund or infinitive form of the verbs.
Then look at page 63 of the Student's
Book to check your answers.

1 Dorian Gray is young and handsome
and detests _____getting_____ (get)
older.

2 'I want _____ (be) young
forever,' he says.

3 Jekyll enjoys _____ (have)
another personality that he can control.

4 The Devil appears in front of Faust, and
suggests _____ (make)
a deal.

5 Faust promises _____
(give) the Devil his soul in return.

6 Viktor Frankenstein imagines
_____ (live) in a world
where people control life and death.

7 He wants to 'play God' and decides
_____ (build) a human
being.

(c) Complete the text with the correct form of the verbs
in the box.

| write help read ~~smoke~~ help fight kill play |

Everyone knows about Sherlock Holmes, the famous
Victorian detective, who enjoyed [1] ___smoking___ his pipe
and practised [2] _____ his violin while he thought
about his latest case. Not so many people are familiar with
his enemy, Professor Moriarty.

Whereas Holmes promised [3] _____ evil, Moriarty
chose [4] _____ it. In fact, Moriarty offered
[5] _____ all the criminals in London.

When Holmes' creator, Sir Arthur Conan Doyle, didn't feel
like [6] _____ any more detective stories, he
decided [7] _____ both characters. In a famous
scene from *The Final Problem* (1893), Moriarty and Holmes
fell to their deaths while
fighting on top of the
Reichenbach waterfalls
in Switzerland.

However, under
pressure from his
readers who missed
[8] _____ about
their favourite detective, Conan
Doyle bought Holmes back to life for 1903's *The Adventure
of the Empty House*. So did Moriarty really die? Only one
man knows.

(d) Put the words in order to make sentences.

1 family / I / really / with / enjoy / time / spending / my
I really enjoy spending time with my family.

2 again / see / I / to / you / hope / soon
_____.

3 see / lesson / to / My / asked / me / the / after /
teacher
_____.

4 called / being / detests / Timothy / He
_____.

5 imagine / I / getting / angry / can't / him
_____.

6 to / more / to / have / patient / learn / You'll / be
_____.

(e) Complete the sentences with a verb from box A and box B in the correct forms.

Box A	Box B
feel like miss practise afford	give go drive buy
decide mind ~~offer~~ promise	live get up study ~~lend~~

1 Dad ___*offered*___ ___*to lend*___ me his car for the weekend. Where shall we go?

2 I really don't _____ _____ to school today. I want to stay in bed all day!

3 I can't _____ _____ a new computer. I've only got 300 Euros.

4 This city's so noisy. I really _____ _____ by the sea.

5 She _____ _____ me her answer tomorrow. I hope she says 'yes'.

6 I have to _____ _____ . I've got my test next week, and I'm really bad at parking!

7 I don't _____ _____ early but I prefer to sleep in at weekends.

8 It was a difficult choice, but I've finally _____ _____ French at university.

2 Vocabulary

Noun suffixes

(a) Write the noun form of the words in the box in the correct column.

> kind   popular   ~~relax~~   protect   prefer   probable   react
> enjoy   prepare   imagine   agree   differ   entertain   possible

-ation	-ence	-ment	-ness	-ion	-ity
relaxation					

(b) Complete the text with the correct form of the words.

James Bond's [1] ___*popularity*___ is as big as it has ever been.   POPULAR

Today's audiences continue to [2] _____ 007 more than   ENJOYMENT

40 years after his first appearance in 1962's *Dr No.*

Bond still offers the world [3] _____ from villains   PROTECT

by using his [4] _____ .   IMAGINE

Young or old, male or female, audiences all [5] _____   AGREEMENT

that Bond films are still great [6] _____ .   ENTERTAIN

3 Pronunciation

Stress in nouns, adjectives and verbs

(a) 🔊 Listen and underline the stressed syllables. In which pairs of words does the stress change?

1	pre<u>pare</u>	prepar<u>a</u>tion	4	lazy	laziness
2	prefer	preference	5	protect	protection
3	enjoy	enjoyment	6	popular	popularity

(b) Practise saying each pair of words.

4 Grammar

Verbs with gerunds or infinitives

a Match the sentences with the pictures. Write a–d in the boxes.

1 I stopped to have a look at the map. ☐

2 I remember posting the letter. ☐

3 I remembered to post the letter. ☐

4 I stopped looking at the map. ☐

a

b

c

d

b Match the questions and the answers.

1	Did you remember to phone Jane?	a	No thanks, I stopped drinking it last year.
2	Do you remember living in France?	b	I'm sorry, I've nearly finished. It's a great computer game!
3	Why are you so late?	c	No, I'll give her a call now.
4	Do you want a cup of coffee?	d	I stopped to buy some milk on the way home.
5	Why don't you stop making that noise?	e	No, I was only two.

c Circle the correct word. Sometimes there is more than one possibility.

1 It's started *to rain* / *raining.*

2 I remember *to meet* / *meeting* Kevin for the first time, five years ago.

3 I hate *to drive* / *driving* at night.

4 He stopped *to eat* / *eating* meat two years ago.

5 I stopped *to buy* / *buying* a CD on my way home.

6 She loves *to go* / *going* out at the weekend.

7 Did you remember *to tell* / *telling* Nigel we can meet him tonight?

8 They began *to work* / *working* at 7 am.

5 Culture in mind

Read the text and mark the statements *T* (true) or *F* (false). Correct the false statements.

STREET ARTS SKATEBOARDING

If graffiti is the art of today's streetwise teenagers, then skateboarding is their sport. Skateboarding has never been more popular. There are an estimated 200,000 skaters in the UK. Most cities and towns have official skate parks. Many are provided by the local council and these are often free. Others are owned by private companies and skaters usually have to pay to use the facilities. Some of these parks, such as the Epic Skate Park in Birmingham and Bones Skate Park in Manchester, are famous throughout the skating world.

Skating has also become big business and there are many companies selling skateboards, skating accessories and fashion items.

Part of the rise of the popularity of skating is because of its inclusion in the extreme sport scene and competitions like the X-games and the urban games offer large money prizes for the winners. Competitors in the events can become very famous in the skating world. Professional skaters like Raphael Brunis from France and Danny Cerezini from Brazil are often sponsored by companies to use their products.

A SKATER'S DICTIONARY

The deck: the main platform area of a skateboard.

Going fakie: travelling backwards on the skateboard.

Goofy: to skate with your right foot forward. The opposite of regular.

Graphics: the art work on the bottom of a deck.

Slam: to fall off your skateboard and hurt yourself.

Stoked: the feeling of doing something well.

1 Skateboarding was more popular in the past. ☐

2 All skate parks in the UK are free. ☐

3 There's a lot of money involved in skateboarding. ☐

4 Competitions like the X-games have encouraged new skaters. ☐

5 Professional skaters are often given money by companies if they use their products. ☐

6 Vocabulary

Belonging to a group

Beckie is a 16-year-old skater. Complete what she says about skating with the words in the box.

| hooked up with   felt left out by   hanging out with   look up to |

I love skating. I love the sensation of moving fast and the danger of knowing that I could slam at any time. But I also love the social side. I love [1] .... other skaters for street sessions. Some of them are fantastic skaters. I really [2] .... them, and I want to be as good as they are one day.

I felt different at school, so I sometimes [3] .... a lot of my classmates but when I [4] .... my skating friends, I found out there were other people who are like me.

Skills in mind

7 Listen

a 🔊 You will hear part of an interview with a film critic about how monsters have changed in films. Listen and tick (✓) the characters he mentions.

Friday 13th: Jason

Frankenstein's Monster

Dracula

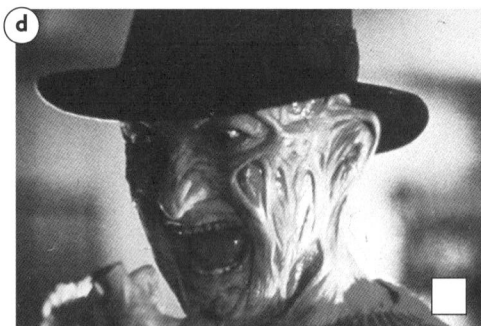

Nightmare on Elm Street: Freddie

b 🔊 Listen again and complete the sentences.

1 People have always been fascinated by monsters and the dark side ....

2 Without evil there is no such thing ....

3 The late .... and early part of the .... was the golden age of the monster.

4 Frankenstein's Monster and Mr Hyde were the results of humans trying to ....

5 .... have no motivation. They're very two-dimensional.

6 Freddie, Jason and Michael Myers are really just three ....

7 Audiences just want to see how many ....

8 All these monsters do is make us scared to go to ....

Listening tip

How to complete sentences

- As with all listening exercises, read through the questions carefully before you listen. This will help prepare you for what you might expect to hear.

- Try to predict what the missing word(s) might be. However, remember that your predictions may be wrong, so you still need to listen carefully to check.

- You will not always hear the exact words that are in the question. Listen carefully for different words that are used that have the same meaning.

  For example, question 1 says:

  People have always been *fascinated by* monsters.

  You heard:

  The human race has always been *extremely interested in* monsters.

- You are only expected to write between one and three words. No more.

- Finally, read through your answers carefully. Make sure they are grammatically correct and check your spelling.

Unit check

1 Fill in the spaces

Complete the text with the words in the box.

> left   hang   vandalism   doing   to do   ~~to get~~   getting   popularity   hooked   shy

I started [1] _to get_ involved with graffiti because I [2] _____ up with Paul. I felt
[3] _____ out by most other kids at school. I was [4] _____ and Paul was the only one who
used to talk to me. We started to [5] _____ out together. Paul was a bit of a rebel and one day he
suggested [6] _____ some spray paint.

I know it was [7] _____ but for six months I sprayed my tag all over town. Then one day I got caught.
I promised my parents I would stop but I really missed [8] _____ it. So I decided [9] _____
something about it. With my headmaster's permission, our school now has a fantastic graffiti wall and my
[10] _____ in the school has never been higher.

`9`

2 Choose the correct answers

(Circle) the correct answers, a, b or c.

1. Stephen Spielberg's films are great. He's got such a good _____ .
   a imagine   b entertainment   c (imagination)

2. I must remember _____ the DVD back to the shop today.
   a taking   b to take   c to bring

3. She's not unfriendly. She's just a bit _____ .
   a shyness   b shy   c friendly

4. That teacher is well known for her _____ .
   a kind   b kindly   c kindness

5. Many teenagers like to hang _____ with their friends in shopping centres.
   a out   b in   c up

6. They don't feel like _____ to the party tonight.
   a going   b to going   c to go

7. My parents don't _____ about anything.
   a agree   b agreement   c agreeing

8. After walking six kilometres, they stopped _____ a drink and a rest.
   a to have   b having   c have

9. I really _____ up to my grandfather. He's an amazing man.
   a see   b watch   c look

`8`

3 Correct the mistakes

In each sentence there is a mistake with the gerund or the infinitive. Underline the mistakes and write the correct sentence.

1. I enjoy <u>to</u> studying English.   _I enjoy studying English._
2. He asked to me go to the party. _____
3. I stopped to work as a teacher last year. _____
4. She's decided studying German in Berlin for a year. _____
5. Did you remember saying 'Happy Birthday' or did you forget? _____
6. I promise tell you as soon as I know. _____
7. I want to learn playing the guitar. _____
8. We can't afford going on holiday this year. _____
9. I suggest to leave an hour earlier. _____

`8`

How did you do?

Total: `25`

| ☺ | Very good 20 – 25 | ☺ | OK 14 – 19 | ☹ | Review Unit 9 again 0 – 13 |

10 Getting into trouble

1 Grammar

Second conditional review

a Match the sentences with the pictures.

1 If we win the World Cup, it will be the best day of my life.

2 If I had my shorts, I would play football.

3 If the rain doesn't stop tomorrow, we won't be able to have a barbeque.

4 If it rained tomorrow, I would be very happy.

5 If you are eighteen, you can come in.

6 If you were eighteen, you could come in.

b Complete the text. Use the correct form of the verbs and *would*, *'d*, *wouldn't* or *might*.

Imagine I ¹ _____found_____ (find) 100 Euros in the street. I'm not sure what I ² _'d do_ (do). If I ³ _____ (take) it to the police station, they ⁴ _____ (not be) interested. If I ⁵ _____ (ask) in the nearest shop, the assistant ⁶ _____ (say) it was hers. If I ⁷ _____ (give) it to a homeless person, they ⁸ _____ (spend) it on beer. If I ⁹ _____ (tell) my friends, they ¹⁰ _____ (want) to spend it and if I ¹¹ _____ (keep) it, I ¹² _____ (feel) guilty.

I hope I never find 100 Euros in the street!

c Put the words in order to make the sentences.

1 your / go / asked / friend / Say / you / best / shoplifting / to
   Say your best friend asked you to go shoplifting. _____.

2 you / fighting / the / saw / Imagine / two / street / men / in
   _____.

3 forgot / really / test / Suppose / to / for / revise / an / you / important
   _____.

4 in / found / you / cinema / Say / 500 Euros / the
   _____.

5 if / borrowed / friend's / and / it / you / What / broke / your / stereo
   _____?

d Write your own answers to the questions in Exercise 1c. What would you do?

1 *I'd tell him I thought it was wrong.*

2 _____ .

3 _____ .

4 _____ .

5 _____ .

2 Vocabulary

Crime

a) Read the descriptions of the crimes and write the names of the crimes in the spaces. Choose from the words in the box.

> burglary joyriding arson shoplifting
> pick-pocketing ~~vandalism~~

1 'Have you seen the church? They've sprayed graffiti all over it.' ___*vandalism*___

2 'They broke a window to get in but they only took the TV and the DVD player.'

   _____

3 'When he was only twelve, he broke into a car and drove it around, just for fun.'

   _____

4 'I was on the bus. I felt a hand and when I looked for my wallet it was gone.'

   _____

5 'The police are treating the fire at the school as suspicious.' _____

6 'Excuse me, could I take a look in your bag?'

   _____

b) Complete the sentences with the words in the box.

> caught wrong into law ~~away~~ crime

1 Sixteen-year-old John's been getting ___*away*___ with shoplifting for two years; until last week when he got _____ with ten CDs hidden in his coat.

2 When Steve was a teenager he was always getting _____ trouble with the police for vandalism, shoplifting and things like that. Now he's 25 and he's committed a more serious _____ – arson. He burned the town library down.

3 Helen knew she was doing something _____ . She knew that going at 140 kph was breaking the _____ but she didn't think she would have an accident. She's OK but four innocent people are in hospital with serious injuries.

c) What punishment do you think each of the people in Exercise 2b should get? Choose from the words in the box.

> pay a fine   be put on probation
> do community service   be sent to prison

1 *John should do 30 hours community service and be put on probation.*

2 _____
   _____ .

3 _____
   _____ .

3 Grammar

I wish / if only

a (Circle) the correct words.

1 I wish I *am* / (*was*) a bit thinner.

2 If only I *could* / *can* go to the party tonight.

3 My sister wishes she *has* / *had* a boyfriend.

4 Daren wishes he *didn't* / *doesn't* spend so much time playing computer games.

5 My dad wishes he *wasn't* / *isn't* so busy.

6 If only she *loves* / *loved* me.

7 I wish I *don't* / *didn't* have so much homework.

8 If only I *know* / *knew* the answer.

b Mike isn't happy. Read what he says and write *wish / if only* sentences.

1 'I can't drive and I don't have a car.'

   He wishes he could drive and he wishes he had a car.

2 'My parents don't understand me.'

   _____ .

3 'My little brother annoys me all the time.'

   _____ .

4 'My computer's broken.'

   _____ .

5 'I don't have enough money to buy a new bike.'

   _____ .

6 'I can't find my house keys.'

   _____ .

7 'I'm too shy to talk to girls.'

   _____ .

c Look at the pictures and write *I wish / if only* sentences for each of the people.

1 *If only I wasn't so hungry.*

2 _____

3 _____

4 _____

5 _____

6 _____

7 _____

8 _____

9 _____

4 Pronunciation

I wish and *if only*

🔊 Listen and repeat. Pay attention to the stress of *if only* and *I wish*.

1 I wish I was somewhere else.
2 If only he loved me.
3 I wish I didn't have so many problems.
4 If only I could go to the party.
5 I wish it was Saturday.
6 If only she understood.

5 Everyday English

(a) Write down the four phrases in the wordsnake.

thewayIseeitandbesidesthat'sagoodpointyouneverknow

1 *the way I see it* _____
2 _____
3 _____
4 _____

(b) Use phrases 1–4 to complete the dialogue.

Steve: Hey, look. I gave her 5 Euros and she's given me change for 10 Euros.

Lucy: You can't keep it.

Steve: What do you mean?

Lucy: Well, I'd give her the money back.

Steve: What! ¹ _____ , she made the mistake. It's not my fault.

Lucy: ² _____ , she might have to pay for her mistake with her own money ³ _____ , it's just not honest.

Steve: I really need the money.

Lucy: But suppose you were the shop assistant. How would you feel?

Steve: ⁴ _____ . You're right, of course. I wish I had more money!

6 Vocabulary

Phrasal verbs with *down*

Use the verbs in the box in the correct form to complete the sentences.

| turn | slow | ~~get~~ | break |

1 I hate all these end-of-term exams. They're really ___*getting*___ me down.

2 It's a great job offer. You'd be crazy to _____ it down.

3 I'm sorry we're late but the car _____ down and we had to get a bus.

4 If he doesn't _____ down, he's going to have an accident. He's driving too fast.

7 Study help

Key word transformations

In this type of exercise you have to rewrite a sentence using a given word so that it means the same. For example:

John is interested in knowing more about astronomy. **(like)**

John _____ know more about astronomy.

● Think carefully about the key word. How does this relate to the sentence? For example, *is interested in* can have a similar meaning to *would like*.

● Is the key word part of a phrasal verb? Is it part of a fixed expression?

● Identify and underline the part of the sentence you need to change. For example, *is interested in knowing*.

● What else do you need to know about the key word? For example, *would like* is followed by the infinitive.

● Think carefully about the tense. Usually both sentences will be in the same tense but be careful with words like *wish* and conditionals when the tense may change.

● Always check your answer carefully for basic mistakes.

Skills in mind

8 Write

(a) Read the composition and put the paragraphs in the correct order. Write 1–4 in the boxes.

> 'There would be less crime on the streets if the minimum age for prison was dropped to 16.' Discuss this statement and give your own opinion.

A If the minimum age for prison was lowered to 16, we would probably see an immediate drop in crime for two reasons. Firstly, many potential teenage criminals might think twice before getting involved if they knew they could go to prison. Secondly, those who continued to commit crimes but got caught would be in prison and unable to cause more trouble. ☐

B I believe the answer to helping solve the problem of teenage crime is in education. Teenage criminals need to be shown that crime does not pay and taught other ways to live. ☐

C Unfortunately, the benefits of such a harsh new law would be temporary. In prison, these teenagers would meet much more experienced criminals and learn new ways to get away with crimes. When they left prison a few years later, the majority of them would be much more dangerous than when they went in. Crime on the street would soon increase again. ☐

D A survey in the UK shows that about 50% of children between the ages of 11 and 17 have broken the law. However, the most serious statistics are those from boys aged 15 to 16 who are involved in serious crimes such as burglary, physical violence and vandalism. ☐1☐

(b) Match the paragraphs with the summaries 1–4. Write A–D in the boxes.

1 Arguments that agree with the title ☐   3 The writer's opinion ☐

2 An introduction ☐   4 Arguments that disagree with the title ☐

Writing tip

Developing a discursive composition (1)

- A useful way to organise discursive compositions is in four paragraphs:
  1 introduction
  2 arguments for or against
  3 arguments against or for
  4 your opinion

- Read the title carefully and decide what your opinion is. Make notes to support your argument.

- Make notes under two headings: for and against. use these for your second and third paragraphs.

- Good ways to start a composition are:

  – Statistics: 'A survey in the UK shows that about 50% of children ...'

  – A question to be answered: 'Why is society so worried about crime?'

  – A statement supporting the title: 'We live in a violent society ...'

(c) Write a composition of about 250 words to answer the question:

'The world would be a better place if people under 40 made the decisions.' Discuss.

Unit check

1 Fill in the spaces

Complete the text with the words in the box.

| would | imagine | caught | down | put | away | can | ~~wish~~ | could | into |

You have an important composition for your History lesson in the morning. It's 10 pm. You [1] _____wish_____ you had started earlier and it's really beginning to get you [2] _____ . Well, [3] _____ you [4] _____ pay 10 Euros to have it done for you and get an A grade. What [5] _____ you do?

Cheating via the Internet is a serious problem for many schools and universities and many students are getting [6] _____ with it. For a small price, students [7] _____ buy work from one of many websites. However, if a student gets [8] _____ , they can get [9] _____ serious trouble. Most schools will [10] _____ the student on probation; many will even expel them.

9

2 Choose the correct answers

(Circle) the correct answers, a, b or c.

1 He _____ the job down because the money wasn't very good.
   a talked   b played   c (turned)

2 If I _____ your help, I would ask you for it.
   a needed   b need   c will need

3 Nobody saw us. I think we've got _____ with it.
   a away   b over   c up

4 My car's _____ down three times this month.
   a gone   b broken   c run

5 My little brother's always _____ into trouble with my parents.
   a being   b going   c getting

6 He didn't slow _____ although the road was wet.
   a down   b up   c over

7 They made him _____ 100 hours of community service for vandalising the old factory.
   a spend   b make   c do

8 If only I _____ have so many problems.
   a didn't   b don't   c not

9 You might go to prison if you _____ the law.
   a do   b make   c break

8

3 Correct the mistakes

In each sentence there is a mistake with the second conditional or *wish / if only*. Underline the mistakes and write the correct sentence.

1 If only I <u>can</u> afford to buy a new TV. *If only I could afford to buy a new TV.*

2 If I lived by the sea, I'll go surfing every day. _____

3 He wishes he is taller. _____

4 If she is an animal, she'd be a horse. _____

5 What would you do, if you failed your exams? _____

6 If only I'm not so tired. _____

7 If I did met Tom Cruise, I'd ask him for an autograph. _____

8 She wishes she works for a different boss. _____

9 I wouldn't do it if you pay me. _____

8

How did you do?

Total: **25**

| ☺ | Very good 20 – 25 | ☺ | OK 14 – 19 | ☹ | Review Unit 10 again 0 – 13 |

11 Two sides to every story

1 Grammar

Linkers of contrast:
however / although / even though / in spite of / despite

a Complete the sentences with the words in the box.

> bought   don't feel like   ~~went~~
> didn't go   feel like   didn't buy

1 Although I wasn't feeling very well, I ____*went*____ to school.

2 Despite the fact it was expensive, I _____ it.

3 Even though it's my birthday, I _____ celebrating.

4 In spite of the fact the sun was shining, we _____ for a picnic.

5 I know it's only nine pm. However, I _____ going to bed.

6 Even though they're my favourite band, I _____ their new CD.

b Look at the pictures. (Circle) the correct answer.

1 The place looks beautiful. *In spite of /* (*However,*) I couldn't live there.

2 *Although / Despite* I usually love horror films, *The Blair Witch Project* was too scary for me.

3 So you haven't done any work, *even though / in spite of* your exams start tomorrow?

4 *Although / However* I can't speak English very well, I can understand American films fine.

5 We had a fantastic holiday *although / in spite of* the rain.

c Write the second sentence so it means the same as the first. Use the word in brackets.

1 Although she doesn't like rock music, she went to the concert. **(despite)**

   She went to the concert, despite
   the fact she doesn't like rock music.

2 We could understand him, even though his accent was very strong. **(in spite of)**

   _____
   _____ .

3 Despite not feeling very hungry, I ate two pieces of cake. **(although)**

   _____
   _____ .

4 The main course was delicious, but the dessert was a bit disappointing. **(however)**

   _____
   _____ .

5 Even though he's not very tall, he plays basketball really well. **(despite)**

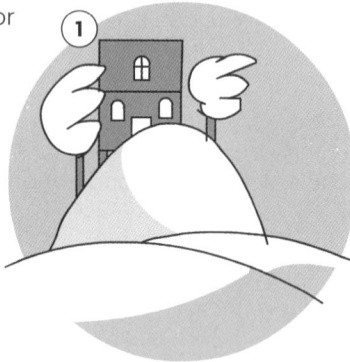

   _____
   _____ .

2 Pronunciation

/əʊ/ *though*

🔊 **Listen and repeat. Pay attention to the sound /əʊ/.**

1 Nobody knows except Joe.
2 Don't drive so slowly in the snow.
3 Even though she didn't go, I enjoyed the show.
4 Although she won't tell me, I already know.

3 Vocabulary

Problems

(a) Complete the sentences with a preposition from the box.

~~up~~   away   over   on   up   out   over   up   back

1 I'll be home late tonight. A problem's *come ___up___ at work.
2 If you've got a problem at school, why don't you *talk it* _____ with your teacher?
3 I can't *make* _____ *my mind* about what to wear tonight.
4 Don't worry about it. I'm sure it'll *go* _____ by itself.
5 I can't give you a decision now. Can I have a few minutes to *think it* _____ ?
6 When nobody knows what to do, Dan always *comes* _____ *with* a great idea.
7 Why don't you *sleep* _____ *it* and give me an answer tomorrow?
8 That's a good point but I'd like to *come* _____ *to it* a bit later.
9 Let's try to *sort* _____ who is doing what before we start.

(b) Complete the text with the correct form of the expressions in *italics* in Exercise 3a.

The problem [1] _____*came up*_____ (appeared) really unexpectedly. It was a simple question but I couldn't [2] _____ (think of) an answer.

I wanted some time to [3] _____ (think about it) but I had to [4] _____ (decide) quickly. It wasn't the sort of problem you needed to [5] _____ (take a lot of time to think about) and there were people waiting behind me.

Maybe I could [6] _____ (discuss it) with the assistant? No, she didn't look very interested.

This was one problem that wasn't going to [7] _____ (disappear) by itself. And I couldn't [8] _____ (return) to it later. I had to [9] _____ (find a solution) now. And then she asked me again, 'Would you like French fries or onion rings with your hamburger?'

4 ## Grammar
Modal verbs of deduction (present)

a Match the two parts of the sentences.

1 He can't be hungry,
2 He must be hungry,
3 He might be hungry,
4 She must know his phone number,
5 She can't know his phone number,
6 She might know his phone number,

a she's his best friend!
b he didn't have a very big lunch.
c he doesn't have a phone!
d he's just eaten two large pizzas!
e she's a friend of his sister's.
f he hasn't eaten for 48 hours!

b Rewrite the sentences so they mean the opposite.

1 It might not be true.   *It might be true.*
2 She must be happy.   _____ .
3 They might speak English.   _____ .
4 You can't like olives!   _____ .
5 They might not know.   _____ .
6 He must live near here.   _____ .

c Complete the sentences with *must*, *can't* or *might*.

1 That plate's just come out of the oven. It _____ be hot.
2 They're speaking Spanish, and I think they're from South America. They _____ be from Peru.
3 She _____ know. It's a secret!
4 I'm not sure what it is. It _____ be some kind of monkey.
5 Everyone passes that exam. It _____ be very difficult.
6 That bird's eating the bananas. It _____ like them!

d Write sentences about the pictures. Use *can't* and *must*.

1 Her boyfriend sends her flowers every day.
   He must love her a lot.

2 They've been walking for two days. They _____ _____ .

3 Hardly anyone came to see them. They _____ _____ .

4 They nearly fell asleep. It _____ .

5 There were cameras everywhere. She _____ .

6 He spent another birthday on his own. He _____ _____ .

5 Fiction in mind

(a) Read another extract from *The Fruitcake Special and other stories* by Frank Brennan. What did Harry find in his pocket? What did he do next? Read the text quickly to find the answers.

In *Finders Keepers*, Harry Chen is a lecturer in archaeology at a university in Singapore. Harry wishes he earned more money so he could fill his life with the beautiful old things he studies. One day, he is cleaning an ancient Chinese pot when he drops it and it breaks. A whistle falls out. Nobody is looking so Harry decides to keep it for himself ...

On his way home, Harry forgot about the clay whistle in his pocket. He stopped for a coffee in a noisy shopping centre. As he searched his pocket for money, he felt the whistle in his pocket. When he had sat at his table he took it out to look at. It was still dirty. He gently cleared away the dirt. There was something written on the whistle. The marks looked like writing. He looked more closely and recognised some old Chinese writing. There was very little of it. All it said was: BE STILL.

Be still? How extraordinary. What did it mean? He looked at the whistle again. It was the kind that one blew from the top, like a football whistle. He wondered if it would still work. The thought came into his mind that he wanted to blow it. He wanted to very much. The whistle had not been blown since it had been placed in the pot all those years before. He would blow it. It was small – it would not make much noise. Nobody would notice. So he put it to his mouth and blew.

To his surprise, the whistle gave a thin, clear note that was louder than he expected.

Then there was silence. Complete silence.

Harry noticed something else, too. Everything was still. Nothing was moving. No noise, no movement.

Nothing.

People who had been walking were frozen in mid-step, like statues. They were as still as photographs.

But they weren't photographs. They were real people. Frozen people. Harry's eyes opened wide with surprise. He couldn't believe it. This should not be happening.

But it was. He looked around and saw frozen smiles, frozen steps, a fly frozen in flight, a ball thrown by a child lay frozen above the hand which was waiting to catch it.

And all the while a total, perfect silence.

(b) Read the text again and (circle) the correct answers, a, b or c.

1 Why did Harry take the whistle out of his pocket?
   A Because he had forgotten about it.
   B Because he wanted to look at it.
   C Because he wanted to clean it.

2 What did Harry notice when he first looked at the whistle?
   A It had some Chinese writing on it.
   B It had the words BE STILL written on it.
   C It was dirty.

3 What kind of sound was Harry expecting the whistle to make?
   A A thin, clear note.
   B A musical tune.
   C A quiet sound.

4 What happened when he blew the whistle?
   A Everything turned to ice.
   B Everything went quiet.
   C Everything turned into statues.

To find out what happens next and how Harry uses his whistle – read the story!

Skills in mind

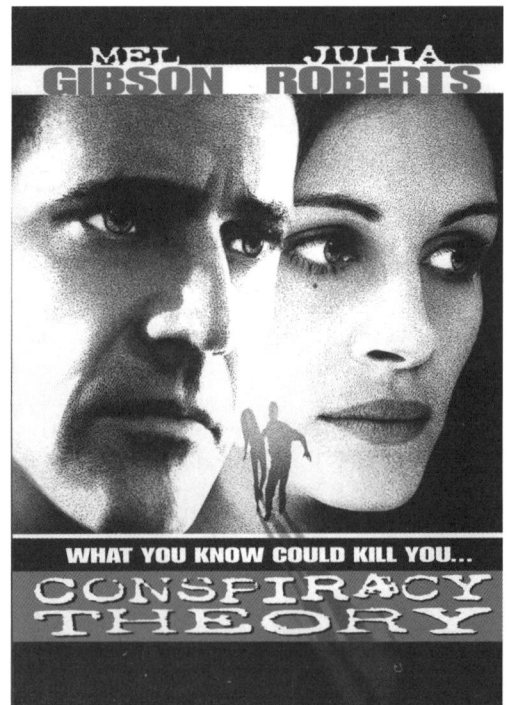

6 Read

Read the film review of *Conspiracy Theory* and choose from the list (A–G) the phrase which best summarises each part (1–6) of the article. There is one extra phrase which you do not need to use.

A   Mad Mel

B   A disappointing ending

C   The man who knows too much

D   The perfect couple

E   A reluctant heroine

F   A villain to remember

G   An exciting love story

films

1

Mel Gibson is Jerry Fletcher, a New York taxi driver with a conspiracy theory for everything. He publishes his ideas on the Internet. One day one of his theories upsets some very powerful men and suddenly his life is in serious danger.

2

The only person who can help him is also the woman he is secretly in love with. Julia Roberts plays Alice Sutton, a justice department lawyer. She wants nothing to do with Fletcher at first but suddenly finds herself drawn into his world.

3

Conspiracy Theory is a well-written, entertaining film which successfully mixes two popular genres. As a thriller, there is plenty of action to keep the audience on the edge of their seats and, as a romance, we end up believing that a top lawyer really could fall in love with a taxi driver.

4

Perhaps the reason for this is in the strength of the acting. Gibson is at his best as the paranoid Fletcher (so paranoid that he keeps his food locked in canisters, locked inside his fridge).

And Julia Roberts reminds us that as well as being one of the most beautiful women on the planet, she is also one of the world's finest actresses.

5

But good as Gibson and Roberts are, the best performance of the film is from *Star Trek's* Patrick Stewart as Dr Jones, a psychologist from a sinister government department. Every minute he is on the screen he leaves the audience wondering what evil he will do next.

6

My only criticism is the last 20 minutes of the film, when director Richard Donner forgets his convincing, tense storyline and the film descends into a traditional good vs. bad shoot-out. Maybe because he's working with Mel Gibson again, Donner suddenly seems to think he's directing the next in his series of *Lethal Weapon* movies.

Reading tip

Matching summaries with paragraphs

- First of all, do not look at the summary phrases to start with. Read the text completely first.

- Think of your own short summary of each part of the text.

- Now read the summary phrases. Do any match your own summaries? Write in the answers.

- Look at the remaining summary phrases carefully. Try and match vocabulary in them to vocabulary in the passage.

- Finally, never leave an answer space empty. If you really have no idea, try to guess.

Unit check

1 Fill in the spaces

Complete the text with the words in the box.

> result   came up   go away   minds   official   ~~conspiracy~~   Although   coming back   Moreover   ignored

From the death of Lady Diana to the UFO crash at Roswell, everybody loves a good [1] _conspiracy_ theory.
[2] _____ most of us forget them quickly, there are some people who dedicate their lives to them.
As a [3] _____ there are now hundreds of webpages on the subject. [4] _____ , books and
films about them are released every year.

Some conspiracy theories won't [5] _____ – they just keep [6] _____ . A survey done in 2003
to mark the 40th anniversary of JFK's death [7] _____ with the amazing statistic that 74% of Americans
don't believe the [8] _____ story. American people have made up their [9] _____ and JFK is
one conspiracy that refuses to be [10] _____ .

9

2 Choose the correct answers

(Circle) the correct answers, a, b or c.

1   Although _____ the nightclub, I don't
   want to go there again.
   a I liking   **b** liking   **c** (I liked)

2   Should I buy the red dress or blue one? I can't
   _____ my mind up.
   a make   **b** decide   **c** do

3   It's not so serious. I'm sure we can
   _____ it out.
   a make   **b** sort   **c** think

4   I decided to travel by train, _____ it
   was more expensive than the bus.
   a despite   **b** even though   **c** however

5   It's boiling today. It _____ be 35°C
   at least.
   a might   **b** must   **c** can't

6   I've got a problem and I want to _____
   it over with you.
   a say   **b** talk   **c** speak

7   _____ knowing a lot about computers,
   she couldn't solve the problem.
   a Despite   **b** However   **c** Although

8   Why don't you _____ on it and make
   a decision in the morning?
   a sleep   **b** relax   **c** lie

9   She didn't go to my party. She _____
   like me very much.
   a can't   **b** must   **c** might

8

3 Correct the mistakes

In each sentence there is a mistake with the linker or the modal verb of deduction. Underline the
mistakes and write the correct sentence.

1   Despite <u>of</u> playing well, they lost.   _Despite playing well, they lost._ _____

2   I don't believe you. That can't to be true. _____

3   I've been working all day. Although I don't feel tired. _____

4   I passed the exam, despite I didn't study for it. _____

5   She must be his wife. He's not married. _____

6   He still loves her, however she's horrible to him. _____

7   It's snowing. It's might be cold outside. _____

8   In spite of knowing not any of the songs, I enjoyed the show. _____

9   She's not a very good artist although she's never had any lessons. _____

8

How did you do?

Total: **25**

| ☺ | Very good
20 – 25 | ☺ | OK
14 – 19 | ☹ | Review Unit 11 again
0 – 13 |

12 Mysterious places

1 Grammar

Indirect questions

a Circle the correct words.

1. I wonder how old *he is / is he*.
2. How old *he is / is he*?
3. I can't tell you where *they're / are they* from.
4. Where *they're / are they* from?
5. I don't understand why *he's / is he* unhappy.
6. Why *he's / is he* unhappy?
7. I don't know what *we're / are we* going to do.
8. What *we're / are we* going to do?

b Look at the pictures and complete the sentences.

1. She wondered _who he was_ .

2. They don't know _____ .

3. He doesn't know _____ .

4. He doesn't understand _____ .

5. The doctor wants to know _____ .

6. She wonders _____ .

Indirect questions and auxiliaries

c Finish the sentences with a full stop or a question mark.

1. They wanted to know when the train left. ....
2. Why are you walking so quickly ......
3. Do you know what I'm thinking ......
4. Where is the nearest police station ......
5. He wondered why she wasn't speaking to him ......
6. I don't know where they are ......
7. What's the problem ......
8. Can you tell me where the toilets are ......

d Complete the questions with the words in the box.

> did she speak to   she spoke to   ~~they live~~
> is it to London   the film starts   do they live
> it is to London   does the film start

1 Can you tell me where
  they live ?

2 Where _____ ?

3 Do you know when _____ ?

4 When _____ ?

5 Do you happen to know who
  _____ ?

6 Who _____ ?

7 Can you tell me how far
  _____ ?

8 How far _____ ?

e Put the words in order to make questions.

1 need / visa / tell / Can / you / me / I / if / a
  Can you tell me if I need a visa?
  _____

2 need / I / visa / Do / a
  _____
  _____ ?

3 went / know / you / Do / they / where
  _____
  _____ ?

4 did / they / go / Where
  _____
  _____ ?

5 you / message / know / to / left / happen /
  if / Do / she / a
  _____
  _____ ?

6 leave / message / she / a / Did
  _____
  _____ ?

7 will / back / you / they / when / Do / know /
  be
  _____
  _____ ?

8 be / When / back / will / they
  _____
  _____ ?

2 Grammar
Modal verbs of deduction (past)

a Circle the correct words.

1 She must have left because her car is *still here / not here.*

2 They can't have played well because they *lost / won.*

3 He must have lost my number because he *phoned / didn't phone* me.

4 You can't have seen my brother because I *have / haven't* got one.

5 We must have done something wrong because he looks really *angry / happy.*

6 I can't have eaten your ham sandwich because I *eat / don't eat* meat.

b Complete the dialogue with the words in the box.

> can't have built   might be   could have built
> must weigh   could have been   don't believe
> must have been   ~~might have used~~

Sally: Wow, look at it. It's amazing. What do you think it was used for?

Brian: The guide says that nobody's sure but they [1] _might have used_ it as an altar where they made sacrifices.

Sally: I think it [2] _____ a big clock using the sun and the shadows.

Brian: You [3] _____ right.

Sally: Do you think that aliens [4] _____ it?

Brian: I [5] _____ that.

Sally: But humans [6] _____ it. Those stones [7] _____ thousands of kilograms.

Brian: But they did build it. Our ancestors [8] _____ more intelligent than we think!

(c) Complete the sentences with *must*, *can't* or *might/could* and the verb.

1 The exam _must have been_ (be) very difficult. Only one person passed.
2 He _____ (leave) the country. He hasn't got a passport.
3 Our dog didn't come home last night. I'm worried a car _____ (run) him over.
4 You _____ (finish) that book! You only bought it yesterday.
5 She _____ (be) really hungry. Did you see how much she ate?
6 I think I _____ (see) this film before but I can't remember.

(d) Complete the sentences with your own ideas.

1 I can't find my wallet. I think I might
   have left it in the shop _____ .

2 Jane looks really excited. She must
   _____ .

3 Did he really say that? He must
   _____ .

4 This band is terrible. They can't
   _____ .

5 She's half an hour late. I think she might
   _____ .

6 He never bought her a present in ten years of marriage. He can't _____
   _____ .

7 Nobody came to his party. He must
   _____ .

8 I'm not sure how he crashed the car. He might
   _____ .

---

3 Pronunciation

must have / might have / can't have / could have / couldn't have

🔊 Listen and complete the sentences.

1 They _____ been disappointed.
2 She _____ left already.
3 I _____ helped you.

4 She _____ gone home.
5 We _____ forgotten to tell him.
6 She _____ seen us.

---

4 Vocabulary

Phrasal verbs

(a) Match the sentence halves.

1 He's the managing director now but he started
2 Her hard work paid
3 She's unhappy because her cat passed
4 I was a bit scared when the lights went
5 We didn't have enough players so we had to call
6 He doesn't really like musicals but we managed to talk

a him into going with us.
b out because it was really dark.
c out as the office boy.
d off and she came first in the exam.
e off the football match.
f away yesterday.

(b) Replace the underlined words with the phrasal verbs in the box.

~~came across~~   passed away   called off   went out   tied in

1 I was reading an old school book and I <u>found</u> my first boyfriend's number written in it. _came across_
2 The police are sure he's <u>connected</u> with the robbery. _____
3 They've <u>cancelled</u> the school party because nobody's interested in it. _____
4 My grandfather <u>died</u> peacefully in his sleep. _____
5 We didn't have any more wood and the fire <u>stopped burning</u>. _____

5 Culture in mind

a World Party were formed by Karl Wallinger. Read his biography and write *one* word in each of the spaces.

W allinger had a musical upbringing. He [1] _____ to the famous Charterhouse music school [2] _____ he studied opera and piano.

From 1983 [3] _____ 1985 he was a member of The Waterboys. [4] _____ the band never found mainstream success, they are still one of the [5] _____ influential bands of the era along with Echo and the Bunnymen and The Smiths.

Karl left The Waterboys [6] _____ 1986 to form World Party. On the first album, *Private Revolution*, he played almost [7] _____ the instruments. It got to number 56 in the UK charts.

In 1990 the second album, *Goodbye Jumbo*, did better by getting to number 39 but more importantly it won the Q award for best album of the year.

Since then the band [8] _____ released a number of CDs which have always received critical praise even if they have never sold [9] _____ copies to make World Party a household name.

In 2000 Karl again tasted success when his song *She's the One* (sung by Robbie Williams) won the Brit award for best single.

b 🔊 Karl Wallinger has won two important awards in his music career. Nowadays there are many different music award ceremonies in the UK to celebrate the music industry. Listen to the descriptions of four of them. Which of the ceremonies do these sentences describe? In the spaces, write:

SH for The Smash Hits T4 Poll Winners Party
MM for The Mercury Music Prize
Q for The Q awards
B for The Brits

1   It only has one award which is chosen by 12 judges. _MM_
2   It has an award for 'The best act in the world.' _____
3   It has awards for the best-looking male and female artists. _____
4   They are considered the Oscars of the British music industry. _____
5   Only four of the awards are chosen by the public. _____
6   It is organised by a music magazine and TV channel. _____

6 Vocabulary

Expressions with *be* + preposition

Circle the correct words.

1   I'm *off / on* chocolate for a while. I'm trying to lose some weight.
2   He's a vegan. He's *past / against* eating any animal product.
3   We're trying to organise a surprise party for Paul but I think he's *on / up* to us.
4   She's *about / over* to have the baby any day now.
5   I don't mind which film we see, it's *up / down* to you.

Skills in mind

7 Write a story (1)

(a) Mark's teacher asked him to write a story ending with the words: *That was the last I ever saw of her*. Read his story quickly. Do you think it answers the question successfully?

The snow [1] *fell / was falling* thick on my windscreen. My eyes were tired from all the whiteness. I wanted to stop but I also wanted to get home. Then I [2] *was seeing / saw* her standing by the side of the road.

She got in quickly. She [3] *shivered / was shivering* from the cold. We soon started talking. She told me that she lived in the next town and then she told me about how her husband [4] *was killed / had been killed* in a car crash on this very road, exactly one year ago.

Then suddenly she [5] *was screaming / screamed* 'Look out!' I looked and saw the car in front of me. I put on the brakes, the car skidded across the road and came to a stop. I [6] *was shaking / shook* with fear. I turned to thank her because she [7] *saved / had saved* my life. However, when I looked round she [8] *went / had gone* and her door was open. I looked out and saw a dark figure [9] *walk / walking* in the distance. It soon disappeared in the snow. That was the last I ever saw of her.

(b) Mark uses a variety of past tenses in his story. (Circle) the correct words.

(c) Write a story ending with the words: *And then the phone rang.*

Unit check

1 Fill in the spaces

Complete the text with the words in the box.

between   have   wonder   might   message   neither   we are   ~~can't~~   must   most

There ¹ _____can't_____ be many people who have never heard of the Bermuda Triangle. This area of sea ² _____ Florida, Bermuda and Puerto Rico is one of the world's ³ _____ mysterious places.

The area is linked with more than 100 lost ships and planes and more than 1,000 deaths. Many of these ⁴ _____ have been because of shipping accidents or tropical storms. But ⁵ _____ of these causes explain the Triangle's most famous mystery, Flight 19.

Flight 19 was a training flight which set off from a US Navy base in Fort Lauderdale. The plane was carrying the most modern technology so the radio operator back at base ⁶ _____ have thought it strange when he received a ⁷ _____ from the pilot complaining that they were lost. He also mentioned that the sea and sky seemed strange. His last communication was: 'I don't know where ⁸ _____ . Looks like we …' They were never seen again. Many people ⁹ _____ why the flight disappeared so suddenly. Others believe it must ¹⁰ _____ been caught in a tropical storm.

| 9 |

2 Choose the correct answers

(Circle) the correct answers, a, b or c.

1 She _____ have enjoyed the film. She left after 20 minutes.
   a must   b might   c (can't)

2 Run! The bomb's _____ to explode.
   a off   b out   c about

3 Do you happen to know where _____ ?
   a they went   b did they go   c went they

4 I was in bed when the lights went _____ .
   a over   b about   c out

5 He might _____ phoned but I wasn't in.
   a has   b had   c have

6 No, thanks, I'm _____ red meat for a while.
   a off   b over   c in

7 I wonder why _____ that.
   a she said   b said she   c did she say

8 I was looking for my keys and I _____ across 10 Euros behind the sofa.
   a found   b came   c went

9 There _____ have been 80,000 people at the game. It was so crowded.
   a can't   b must   c might

| 8 |

3 Correct the mistakes

In each sentence there is a mistake with the questions or the modal of deduction. Underline the mistakes and write the correct sentence.

1 Do you know is he married?   _Do you know if he is married?_ _____

2 Can you tell me when is the next train to Liverpool? _____

3 I can't find it anywhere. She can't have taken it with her. _____

4 They might had been speaking Polish. _____

5 Nobody's sure what did really happened. _____

6 I don't understand why would he say a thing like that. _____

7 She had six children and no husband. Life must have been easy for her. _____

8 I don't know what can we do. _____

9 Do you happen to know when will he get home? _____

| 8 |

How did you do?

Total: | 25 |

| ☺ | Very good 20 – 25 | ☺ | OK 14 – 19 | ☹ | Review Unit 12 again 0 – 13 |

13 Love

1 Grammar

Reported statements review

a Write the sentences in direct speech.

1 The man told the woman that he was really scared of dogs.

   '*I'm really scared of dogs,*' the man told her.

2 Sue told her father that she would go to the cinema with him on Saturday.

   '_____,' Sue told her father.

3 John explained he had to get up early in the morning to catch the train.

   '_____,' explained John.

4 Janet told us there had been an earthquake in China.

   '_____,' Janet told us.

5 Dad said he was sorry he couldn't get home earlier.

   '_____,' said Dad.

6 Ben told us he was going to France in the morning.

   '_____,' Ben told us.

7 Anna said she had to leave before eight o'clock.

   '_____,' said Anna.

8 Marek said that he couldn't type very fast.

   '_____,' said Marek.

b Rewrite the sentences so that they have a similar meaning. Use the word given without changing it.

1 'You must buy your girlfriend some flowers,' Mum said.

   that
   Mum _told me that I had to buy_ some flowers for my girlfriend.

2 'Tony is my brother, not my boyfriend,' Anne said.

   was
   Anne _____ her brother, not her boyfriend.

3 'I have not stolen the money,' the man said.

   said
   The man _____ the money.

4 'I can't go on holiday in August,' Tony said.

   explained
   Tony _____ on holiday in August.

5 'I have not learned anything for the test,' Jane said to us.

   told
   Jane _____ anything for the test.

6 'I'm going to marry Cathy,' Nick said.

   he
   Nick told us that _____ .

7 'I don't want to hear complaints all the time,' the headmaster said.

   said
   The headmaster _____ hear complaints all the time.

8 'I promise to give you the money back in three days' time,' he said to me.

   would
   He promised that he _____ the money back in three days' time.

2 Grammar

Reported questions review

(a) Put the questions into reported speech.

1 'When is your birthday?' (The girl wanted to know ...)
The girl wanted to know when my birthday was.

2 'Will we get to the concert on time?' (Jane asked ...)
....

3 'Can you install this game for me?' (Carol asked me ...)
....

4 'Why can't I stay up longer?' (My little sister asked ...)
....

5 'Where's the hospital?' (The driver wanted to know ...)
....

6 'Have you been to Canada?' (He asked me ...)
....

(b) Complete the conversation with the phrases in the box.

> don't think   was brilliant   doesn't mean   I'll go
> ~~Have you seen~~   Why's that   it was awful

Lucy: [1] *Have you seen* Matrix Revolutions?

Liz: No, I haven't, but I [2] .... I'd want to.

Lucy: [3] .... ?

Liz: My friends have seen it, and they said
[4] ....

Lucy: I find that surprising. I've only seen the first part, and that [5] ....

Liz: I know, but that [6] .... much!

Lucy: You're probably right, but I think
[7] .... and see it anyway.

(c) Complete the report on the conversation between Lucy and Liz.

Lucy asked Liz [1] *whether she had seen* Matrix Revolutions. Liz replied that she [2] .... ,
but she [3] .... want to. Lucy
[4] .... to know why. Liz replied that her friends [5] .... it, and they
[6] .... awful. Lucy answered that she
[7] .... that surprising. She
[8] .... the first part, and that
[9] .... brilliant. Liz replied that she
[10] .... , but that [11] .... much.
Lucy replied that she [12] .... right, but she
[13] .... and see it anyway.

3 Vocabulary

Appearance

Robert

Jenny

Donna

Kevin

(a) Write the names of the people.

1 Who is overweight? ...... *Kevin* ......
2 Who has got a ponytail? ....
3 Who has got a double chin?
....
4 Who has got wrinkles on his forehead?
....
5 Who is clean shaven? ....
6 Who has got a mole on her cheek?
....

(b) Complete the sentences.

1 Robert has got ...... *spots* ...... on his face.
He is rather short, but ....

2 Jenny has got .... hair. She is slim, but she has got a .... chin.

3 Donna has got her hair in a ....
On her left arm, she's got a .... of a dolphin.

4 Kevin has got .... eyebrows.
He has got .... hair,
a .... and .... on his forehead.

4 Vocabulary

Personality

Complete the text. Circle the correct answers, a, b, c or d.

I have three sisters and two brothers. My oldest brother is Adam. Once I was ill for two weeks. Adam was really [1] _____ and looked after me very well. But sometimes Adam is really [2] _____ . He likes to tell us what to do all the time and how we should do it. We often tell him to be more [3] _____ , but he doesn't listen. Ernest, my other brother, is the most [4] _____ of us all. He was always the best student in his class, and he finished university really quickly. The problem is that he never has any time for himself, but we tell him to be a little less [5] _____ and relax a bit more. We all get on really well with my youngest sister Margaret, except when we try to interfere with her life. She is a very [6] _____ person, and doesn't like other people to tell her what to do.

	a		b		c		d	
1	a	sympathetic	b	ambitious	c	determined	d	imaginative
2	a	sensitive	b	independent	c	bossy	d	ambitious
3	a	imaginative	b	bossy	c	ambitious	d	considerate
4	a	bossy	b	ambitious	c	sympathetic	d	insensitive
5	a	determined	b	imaginative	c	sensitive	d	considerate
6	a	independent	b	insensitive	c	considerate	d	sympathetic

5 Grammar

Reporting verbs

a **Circle the correct verbs.**

Tracey and Caroline were talking about going to the cinema. Tracey [1] *said* / told that she [2] *wanted* / *wants* to see a thriller. Caroline [3] *said* / *told* that she [4] *will* / *would* like to see a romantic film. Tracey [5] *said* / *offered* to go and get a programme. Caroline [6] *suggested* / *asked* checking the programme on the Internet. She went online, but some minutes later she [7] *said* / *told* that there [8] *aren't* / *weren't* any interesting films on. Tracey [9] *said* / *told* Caroline that it [10] *might* / *will* be better to rent a DVD and watch it at home. So Caroline [11] *asked* / *said* her to go and get a good DVD. Tracey [12] *said* / *told* that she [13] *is* / *was* happy to do that. Twenty minutes later she came back. She [14] *apologised* / *complained* for choosing a thriller, but Caroline [15] *refused* / *invited* to watch it!

b **Use the past form of the verbs in the box to write the sentences in reported speech.**

explain ~~tell~~ refuse persuade beg suggest agree apologise

1 'Wash your hands before you sit down!' Mum said to my little brother.
   Mum told my little brother to wash his hands before he sat down.

2 'Please, please lend me your DVD player!' Pete said to me.
   _____ .

3 'I'm really sorry that I forgot about your birthday,' Cathy said to her dad.
   _____ .

4 'All right – I'll make pizza for supper,' my mother said.
   _____ .

5 'I'm late because of the traffic,' she said. _____ .

6 'I won't do it!' she said. _____ .

7 Tom: 'I know you don't like football, but please will you watch the match with me, just for once?'
   Alan: 'Oh, OK then. But just this once!'
   Tom _____ .

8 'Let's play tennis,' said Lucy.
   _____ .

6 Culture in mind

a Complete the text with the correct form of the words.

A traditional Greek Cypriot wedding has many
1 .... to a Church of England wedding. SIMILAR

One example is that it takes between 40 minutes and an hour, and the bride wears a white dress and the groom wears a black suit. But one big
2 .... is that the service is usually DIFFERENT
3 .... for by the bridesmaids. PAY
During the service the couple exchange rings and put a type of crown on each other's heads to show that they are King and Queen for the day.

Afterwards, there is a big **4** .... RECEIVE
for all the family and guests, with lots of
5 .... Greek music and plenty of TRADITION
6 ...., including the 'money dance', DANCE
when guests pin money onto the couple's clothes to wish them **7** .... in their future HAPPY
life together. The guests also break plates on the floor for good luck!

b Read the sentences. Write *T* (true) or *F* (false).

1 Greek Cypriot weddings are exactly the same as Church of England weddings. ☐

2 The groom and the bride wear lots of different colours. ☐

3 The bride and groom give each other rings. ☐

4 They put crowns on each other's heads. ☐

5 The 'money dance' is the only dance at the party. ☐

6 Guests put money into the pockets of the bride and groom. ☐

7 Breaking plates is supposed to bring good luck. ☐

7 Pronunciation
Intonation in reported questions

a 🔊 Listen and repeat.

1 What's your favourite colour?
2 How are you enjoying the meal?
3 When will you be back?
4 Do you often watch TV?

b 🔊 Listen and repeat.

1 He asked me what my favourite colour was.
2 We asked them how they were enjoying the meal.
3 He asked her when she'd be back.
4 He asked me if I often watched TV.

8 Vocabulary
Relationships

Complete the sentences with the words in the box.

| broken-up | engaged | getting back | married |
| falling in love | married | going out | divorced |

1 Jane and Benjamin have __*broken up*__ . He is .... with another girl.

2 My parents got .... fourteen years ago. Ten years later they got .... , and now they are thinking of .... together again.

3 I think Sandra is .... with Chris. She's been looking at him all evening!

4 Bruce and Nancy have been .... for three years but they still haven't said when they're getting ....

Skills in mind

9 Read

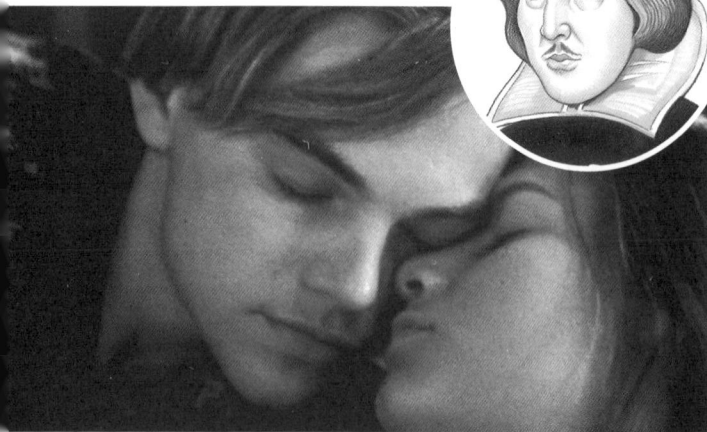

Read the article. For each question (circle) the correct answer, a, b or c.

Romeo and Juliet
the greatest love story of all times

Since the invention of the motion picture in 1894, *Romeo and Juliet* has been one of the most popular stories in films. Numerous movies have been based on Shakespeare's famous love story, the earliest dating back to 1900.

Many directors have taken this famous play and made it into a film, trying to keep to the themes of the original story.

One of them is Baz Luhrmann. His version of *Romeo and Juliet*, produced in 1996, has been described as an original, post-modern version of Shakespeare's tragic love story.

With this extremely successful film, Luhrmann has managed to update the story – by combining modern-day settings and characters with almost the original language. The story is set in Miami. The changes in the language, together with dramatic gun fights and passionate love scenes, make the story more accessible to modern audiences.

In Luhrmann's version of the film, the main characters, Romeo (Leonardo di Caprio) and Juliet (Clare Danes), are Miami teenagers of the nineties. Even though the setting of the film is very unconventional, it contains all the themes of the original version, because it does not change the story at all.

Reading tip

How to answer multiple choice questions

In Unit 7 you got some ideas on how to do multiple choice questions with listening. When you do them with reading, keep the following in mind.

- Read the whole text first, but pause after each paragraph. Ask yourself two questions:
  1 What's the main idea in the paragraph that I've just read?
  2 What might the next paragraph be about?
     Thinking in this way while you are reading will later help you find the answers to the questions more easily.

- Some of the answers to multiple choice questions use words or phrases from the text. Be careful – they might be the wrong answers! Look at the multiple choice questions in Exercise 9. Which answers contain language from the text, but are clearly wrong?

- You will not always find the correct answer to a question directly from the text. Some questions ask for your ability to draw conclusions from what you are reading. Read the questions below again. Which ones can't be answered directly from the text?

1 Lots of films have been produced that are based on
   a William Shakespeare's play *Romeo and Juliet*.
   b a motion picture from 1894 called *Romeo and Juliet*.
   c an invention made by William Shakespeare in 1894.

2 Baz Luhrmann
   a is the only film director who has tried to keep to the themes of the original play.
   b is one of the film directors who have tried to keep to the themes of the original play.
   c produced his earliest version of *Romeo and Juliet* as early as 1900.

3 The language in Luhrmann's film is
   a exactly the same as in Shakespeare's play.
   b completely different from Shakespeare's play.
   c almost the same as in Shakespeare's play.

4 Why did Luhrmann make some changes to the setting?
   a Because he added gun fights and passionate love scenes.
   b Because he wanted to help people to understand the story better.
   c Because teenagers in Miami speak a very strong dialect.

5 Which of the following statements is true about Baz Luhrmann?
   a He produced a successful, but unconventional and provocative version of the play.
   b He produced a modern, but not very successful version of the play.
   c He produced a successful modern version of the play.

Unit check

1 Fill in the spaces

Complete the text with the words in the box.

~~slim~~ cropped bad-tempered sympathetic hair tattoo fit ambitious determined ponytail

My best friend's name is Carolyn. A year ago she started to exercise regularly, and now she is really [1] _slim_ . She also changed her hairstyle. First she had long [2] _____ which she wore in a [3] _____ , but now her hair is [4] _____ . Carolyn is the best student in my class. She is really [5] _____ , and sometimes she gets a bit [6] _____ when she doesn't get top marks. But I like Carolyn a lot. When I have a problem, she is very [7] _____ . I want to learn from Carolyn. I am going to exercise regularly too. I am very [8] _____ and will not give up before I am as [9] _____ as her. But one thing is for sure. I am not going to get myself a [10] _____ on my left arm. That's something I don't like so much about her!

| 9 |

2 Choose the correct answers

(Circle) the correct answers, a, b or c.

1 Jane said that she _____ nervous.
   a (was) b were c be

2 Your sister said that she _____ to leave.
   a had b having c have

3 John promised that he _____ study the words.
   a to b would c would to

4 They asked me if I _____ seen their dog.
   a have been b having c had

5 They wanted to know when he _____ back.
   a would come b will coming c would

6 I asked them if they _____ help me.
   a be able to b able c could

7 They apologised for not _____ on time.
   a being b to be c been

8 We asked them _____ us an email.
   a writing b write c to write

9 I suggested _____ Peter for some advice.
   a asking b to ask c ask

| 8 |

3 Correct the mistakes

In each sentence there is a mistake with vocabulary (relationships), reported speech, a reported question or a verb pattern in reported speech. Underline the mistakes and write the correct sentence.

1 Jane and Tony got <u>divorcing</u>. *Jane and Tony got divorced.* _____

2 It seems Cathy is falling love with Nick. _____

3 Is it true that your sister and her husband have broken down? _____

4 Nick persuaded me coming to his party. _____

5 Jane told Martin going out. _____

6 I asked her come to my party. _____

7 She asked me what was my favourite food. _____

8 I promised that I would be not late again. _____

9 She said that she not had stolen the money. _____

| 8 |

How did you do?

Total: | 25 |

| 😊 | Very good 20 – 25 | 😐 | OK 14 – 19 | 😞 | Review Unit 13 again 0 – 13 |

14 Anger

1 Grammar

Third conditional review

(a) Match the sentences with the pictures a–d. Write 1–4 in the boxes.

1 If she'd studied harder for the test, she would have got a better mark.
2 If they'd built a better road, there wouldn't have been so many accidents.
3 If it hadn't been so muddy, they wouldn't have got so dirty.
4 He wouldn't have driven so fast if he'd known that the policeman was there.

(b) Complete the third conditional sentences with the correct form of the verbs.

1 I don't think so many people _would have come_ (come) to the concert if they _'d known_ (know) that the lead singer was ill.
2 What _____ you _____ (say) if I _____ (show) you the present earlier?
3 We _____ (save) a lot of money if we _____ (go) to a cheaper restaurant.
4 He _____ (not buy) such an expensive guitar if his father _____ (not give) him the money.
5 If she _____ (pass) her driving test, she _____ (drive) us to Italy.
6 No one _____ (hear) us if we _____ (not shout).
7 If you _____ (not run after) me, I _____ (not fall).
8 Why _____ he _____ (phone) us if he _____ (not be) in trouble?

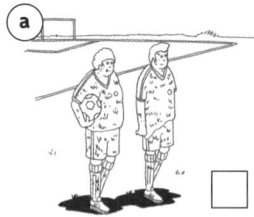

(c) Match the sentences below with the pictures a–g. Write 1–7 in the boxes. Then join the sentences using the third conditional.

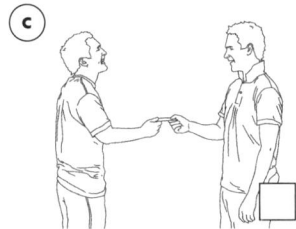

1 One of Daniel's friends gave Daniel his ticket for a concert.
2 Daniel went to the concert.
3 He stood next to a girl called Annie.
4 Annie and Daniel had a chat.
5 The next evening, Daniel and Annie went to a disco.
6 They fell in love.
7 A year later they got married.

If one of Daniel's friends hadn't given Daniel his ticket, he wouldn't have gone to the concert.
If Daniel hadn't gone to ...

2 Grammar

I wish / if only for past situations

Write down a regret for each situation, starting your sentences with *I wish* or *If only*.
Use an expression from the box for each sentence.

| kick ball | drive so fast | break vase | play with pen | ~~slam door~~ | buy sports car |

1 *I wish I hadn't slammed*
  the door .
  The neighbours are really annoyed.

2 _____
  _____ .
  Where can I buy a new one now?

3 _____
  _____ .
  What will my parents say?

4 _____
  _____ .
  I'll never get rid of the stain on
  my jeans!

5 _____
  _____ .
  This is going to cost me money.

6 _____
  _____ .
  I have no money left.

3 Grammar

should have / shouldn't have (done)

a Match the two parts of the sentences.

1 I should listen to my parents
2 I should have listened to my parents
3 I shouldn't have been angry with Jane
4 I shouldn't be angry with Jane
5 I should write her an email
6 I should have written her an email

a because I think they were right.
b because it wasn't her fault.
c before it is too late.
d because I think they are right.
e before it was too late.
f because it isn't her fault.

b Write a response to these statements using *should have* or *shouldn't have* plus a phrase from the box with the correct verb form.

| ~~leave earlier~~ | call the police | take a jumper with her | take the risk | wear better shoes | buy something earlier |

1 I missed the bus. *You should have left earlier.* _____

2 She's feeling cold. _____

3 He lost all his money. _____

4 They can't find a present for their mum. _____

5 They saw that the man had a gun. _____

6 He slipped on the pavement and broke his leg. _____

4 Pronunciation

should have / shouldn't have

a 🔊 Listen and repeat.

1 You (shouldn't have) done that.
2 I shouldn't have listened to her.
3 I gave it back to her, but I shouldn't have.
4 We should have bought it.
5 They didn't tell us, but they should have.
6 You should have written to me.

b 🔊 Listen again. (Circle) *should have* and *shouldn't have* when *have* is weak and sounds like /əv/. Underline *shouldn't have* and *should have* when it is pronounced more fully.

5 Vocabulary

Anger

Complete the text. (Circle) the correct answers, a, b, c or d.

A few weeks ago I wanted to go on a bike tour with three friends. The evening before the tour Jeremy and Laura called to say they couldn't come. I was ¹ _____ ! I was especially ² _____ with Jeremy because he was the one who had suggested going for the bike tour. Anyway, the next morning I was sorry for losing my ³ _____ and rang up Jeremy to apologise. But he didn't even want to talk. He was just ⁴ _____ ! I ⁵ _____ my cool and said, 'OK. If you are so ⁶ _____ and lose your temper that easily, it's your problem and not mine!' You know what? He started having ⁷ _____ and bit ⁸ _____ for 'shouting at him'! I don't know what he meant! But what could I do? I think I can only ⁹ _____ and wait for him to cool down again!

1 a (furious)	b hot-headed	c mad at	d calm
2 a hot-headed	b temper	c cross	d calm
3 a head	b tantrum	c calm	d temper
4 a cool	b hot-headed	c calm	d furious
5 a got	b had	c bit	d kept
6 a cross	b calm	c cool	d hot-headed
7 a a temper	b a real tantrum	c my head off	d his cool
8 a my head off	b a real tantrum	c his cool	d his temper
9 a stay calm	b have a tantrum	c be cross	d bite his head off

6 Everyday English

Use one of the phrases in the box to complete each space in the dialogue.

there's something I want to say   the thing is   in that case   what I mean is

Julie: Hey, Diana. What's up?

Diana: Well, I'm a bit sad today.

Julie: But I've heard you're going out with Jamie? Isn't that great?

Diana: Well, ¹ _____ , I'm a bit worried.

Julie: Is there a problem?

Diana: I should have listened to Sarah, she warned me. ² _____ , I shouldn't have trusted Jamie.

Julie: Why's that?

Diana: Sarah says he's saying bad things about me! I wish I'd known, I would never have gone out with him.

Julie: ³ _____ , Diana.

Diana: What's that?

Julie: Sarah would like to go out with Jamie herself. Talk to him. I'm sure you two can work it out. Maybe he hasn't even said those things ...

Diana: Mmm. ⁴ _____ , I'll try to talk to him. Thanks Julie!

Study help

How to complete cloze texts

Sometimes you have to fill in the spaces in a text with one word and no clues are given.

- It's important that you read the whole text first. Don't focus on the spaces – try to understand what the general meaning of the text is. Look at the title too!

- Carefully study the words before and after the space. Try to find clues that help you to identify the meaning of the word needed. Is it the opposite of something? Is it an example of something? Is it a synonym? Is it part of an expression?

- Try to identify the type of word that's needed. For example, is it an article? A preposition? A noun? Look at number 2 in the text below. The words before the space are: *can be caused*. This tells us that the sentence is a present simple passive construction. The words after the space tell us what the cause is, so what is the missing word?

- If the word you need to fill in is a verb, make sure it agrees with the subject that it goes with. Don't forget the third person *s*!

- If you are not sure about a word, try to guess the answer and note it down on a piece of paper. Then come back later to the spaces you found difficult to do. You will sometimes find it easier to find the right word the second time round.

- Read the whole text again and check that the words you have filled in make sense.

Complete the text with one word for each space.

What is **anger?** And what can you do about it?

According to psychologists, anger [1] _is_ a feeling. As with other emotional states, we notice changes when we are angry. There are biological changes, for example. Our heart rate and blood pressure go up, as do the levels of our energy hormones.

Anger can be caused [2] _____ both external and internal events. You could be angry at a specific [3] _____ , such as a classmate or a teacher, or perhaps an event. For example, maybe you have [4] _____ your bus, or it starts raining and you [5] _____ planned to go for a walk. Or your anger could be caused by worrying [6] _____ your personal problems. Memories of very negative events can also trigger angry feelings.

However, you can control your angry feelings with simple techniques. There are books and courses [7] _____ can teach you relaxation techniques, and once you have learned the techniques you can use them in different situations. If you are in a relationship where both of you are quick-tempered, it might be a good idea for both of you [8] _____ learn these techniques. Practise these techniques daily and learn to use [9] _____ when you're in a difficult situation.

Skills in mind

8 Write a story (2)

(a) John's teacher asked him to write a story with the title: 'An embarrassing situation'.
Read his answer. Why was the situation embarrassing?

An embarrassing situation

I was on holiday with two of my friends and we were staying in a hotel.[1] The football world cup was starting and we all wanted to watch it. We decided to watch it in my room, because there was a TV there, but we just couldn't get a picture. We tried everything but we couldn't sort it out.[2]

Finally,[3] we decided to phone someone in reception and ask them to look at it. When the man arrived, he looked at the TV and calmly switched it on, before taking the remote control and pressing the button for the right channel![4]

(b) The writer gives the events, but the text does not contain much detail, so it isn't very interesting. Read the question prompts. Think of answers to them and write them down.

1 Where was the holiday? When? What was the place like? What was the hotel like?

2 How did you feel when you noticed that the TV didn't work? Why?

3 How long did you wait before you called reception? Had the match already started?

4 How did you feel when you realised you hadn't noticed the TV was not switched on? Did you later tell your friends about what had happened? Why / Why not?

(c) Rewrite the text using the ideas you wrote in Exercise 9b to make it more interesting.

(d) Write a story entitled 'A dangerous journey'.

Writing tip

Developing your ideas to write a story (2)

In Unit 12 you were given the last line of a story and asked to complete the story. Here you are given the title.

- Don't start writing without having a clear plan of what you are going to write.

- Develop the storyline first. Have you ever been on a dangerous journey? Has someone you know told you about a dangerous journey?

- If you don't have a story, try to invent one. First of all write the storyline. How does it begin? How does it develop? How does it end?

- Include interesting details, but not too many!

Unit check

1 Fill in the spaces

Complete the letter with the words in the box. There may be more than one possibility.

furious ~~letter~~ keep regretting hot-headed difficult temper work tantrum cross

Dear Jane

Thank you for your ¹ ____letter____ . I'm afraid it's really not very easy to advise you.

You had a fight with your boyfriend and lost your ² _____ , and now you are ³ _____

it. You say in your letter that your boyfriend is quite a ⁴ _____ person, but it seems that it is

_____ for you to ⁶ _____ your cool too. Now you are ⁷ _____ with

him, but maybe you should understand that he is also ⁸ _____ with you? Perhaps you could learn

to relax a bit more and avoid having a ⁹ _____ when you are arguing with someone you like.

Talk to him. Maybe you can ¹⁰ _____ something out together.

Yours, Barbara

| 9 |

2 Choose the correct answers

Circle the correct answers, a, b or c.

1   If I _____ ill, I would have gone to school.
    a (hadn't been)   b were not   c am not

2   They wouldn't _____ in love if they hadn't met.
    a fall   b had fallen   c have fallen

3   If the police hadn't come, the man would have
    _____ .
    a escaping   b escaped   c escape

4   He's going to hit you! Look _____ !
    a in   b out   c under

5   I'm so curious. I wish I _____ her before.
    a asked   b been asked   c had asked

6   I missed the bus. I _____ left so late.
    a hadn't   b should have   c shouldn't have

7   We should have left before they _____ .
    a arrived   b would arrive   c arrive.

8   This is so complicated, I don't think we can
    _____ it out.
    a sort   b stop   c avoid

9   I am so full! If only I _____ so much.
    a not eaten   b wouldn't have eaten
    c hadn't eaten

| 8 |

3 Correct the mistakes

In each sentence there is a mistake with a third conditional, *wish / if only*, *should have done* or a phrasal verb. Underline the mistakes and write the correct sentence.

1   I would have been happy if you <u>would have helped</u>.   *I would have been happy if you had helped.*

2   If they had asked me, I would have not told them. _____

3   If only I known about the problem before! _____

4   I'm tired. I wish I hadn't work so much. _____

5   We should told her before she phoned. _____

6   We should have left before it gets dark. _____

7   I wish she had be here, then we could have discussed it. _____

8   They had a big argument and fell up. _____

9   Please don't worry, I'm sure we can work something in. _____

| 8 |

How did you do?

Total: | 25 |

| ☺ Very good 20 – 25 | ☺ OK 14 – 19 | ☹ Review Unit 14 again 0 – 13 |

15 Fear

1 Grammar

Non-defining relative clauses (giving extra information)

a Complete the sentences with the correct relative clause from the box.

where her family have a restaurant	which I read five times	which is not far from San Francisco	which was why I couldn't go to school
who is still very popular	which I know I wrote down	~~where you can find beautiful beaches~~	whose name I have forgotten

1 I love going on holiday to Ireland, *where you can find beautiful beaches.*

2 Madonna, ... , had her first hit in the 1980s.

3 Karen's best friend, ... , comes from China.

4 She lives in London, ...

5 I had a nasty cold, ...

6 *The Lord of the Rings*, ... , is my favourite book.

7 He is Californian and was born in Santa Cruz, ...

8 I've lost your address, ...

b Complete the text with *who*, *whose*, *which* or *where*.

MARK O'BRIAN, [1] ......*who*...... **was on his way to work early last Tuesday morning, was driving down North Lane when he was shocked by something he saw.**

A driver, [2] .... must have driven down the same street only a few minutes before, had lost control of his car. The car, [3] .... had landed on its roof, burst into flames immediately.

Mr O'Brian, [4] .... quick thinking helped save the driver's life, got out of his car and saw that there was a man in the driver's seat. Mark phoned the fire brigade and then ran back to his own car, [5] .... he kept a fire extinguisher. He rushed back to the scene just as another man was approaching.

O'Brian and the other man, [6] .... has not been seen since the accident, managed to put out the fire.

They then broke the passenger window with a stone and freed the driver, [7] ....

luckily was not seriously injured. He was taken to hospital, [8] .... his condition has been described as 'comfortable'.

c) Join the sentences using *who*, *which*, *where* or *whose*. Sometimes you will need to change the order of the clauses.

1   Joanne speaks six languages. She lives next door.
   Joanne, who lives next door, speaks six languages.

2   I love scuba diving in the Indian Ocean. You can still find a lot of attractive fish there.

   ....

3   Next month Stephanie will move to London. Her partner has a flat there.

   ....

4   Alex is getting married next year. His sister studies with me.

   ....

5   Barbara works as a secretary for Jo & Co. She has won the lottery.

   ....

6   My new computer is fantastic. I got it for a very good price.

   ....

2   Grammar and pronunciation
Defining vs. non-defining relative clauses

a) Write a tick (✓) if the sentence is correct. If the sentence is wrong, write a cross (✗) and insert the commas.

1   Paris which is visited by millions of tourists every year is famous for its art.   ✗
   Paris, which is visited by millions of tourists every year, is famous for its art. .

2   That's the place that I was talking about.   ✓

   ....

3   Let's meet at the shop where your dad works.   ☐

   ....

4   Is that the girl who wrote you a love letter?   ☐

   ....
   ....

5   I live in Green Street where there are two new cinemas.   ☐

   ....
   ....

6   Thank you for your email which I read last night.   ☐

   ....
   ....

7   My dad works in *Tops* restaurant which is famous for its seafood.   ☐

   ....
   ....

8   He is the man whose daughter won the lottery.   ☐

   ....
   ....

b) 🔊 Listen to the sentences in Exercise 2a and check your answers. Where can you hear the pauses?

c) 🔊 Listen again and repeat the sentences.

3   Vocabulary
Adjectives with prefixes

Complete the text with the correct forms of the adjectives. Sometimes the adjective stays the same.

I have a story to tell. I know it will sound [1] *unbelievable* , but it's true. It happened three years ago, when I was a university student. I was waiting outside the library for my girlfriend. She was late, and I was already getting a little [2] .... We had agreed to go to Joe's Café. It was very [3] .... , and it was quite old, but for people like me and my girlfriend it seemed the most [4] .... place to meet. We both liked Joe. He made fun of us, but was never [5] .... or [6] .... The place was clean, and it was also [7] .... , which was great as we were poor students! So in fact my girlfriend Juanita and I were [8] .... guests there.

BELIEVE

PATIENT

FORMAL

LOGICAL

POLITE

HELPFUL EXPENSIVE

REGULAR

In the end, tired of waiting, I went to Joe's Café alone. When I got there, it had gone! It seemed [9] .... , but where the café had been was an empty space. I have never seen Juanita again. And I have never seen Joe again either.

POSSIBLE

4 Grammar

Definite, indefinite and zero article

a Complete the sentences with *the, a, an* or nothing.

1 I go to _____the_____ cinema at least once a week.

2 This is _____ new school that I told you about.

3 His brother works as _____ pilot for British Airways.

4 If he doesn't feel better tomorrow, we'll have to take him to _____ hospital.

5 Lidia plays _____ drums in a band.

6 Can you pass me _____ sugar, please?

7 When does _____ school start?

8 I'm allergic to _____ cats.

b Write a tick (✓) if the line is correct. If the line has an article (*a, an* or *the*) which should not be there, write the word in the space.

Yesterday my friend Linda and I had lunch at the pizzeria	1	✓
behind our school. I know Linda is not keen on ~~the~~ pizzas,	2	*the*
but I think she came along because of me. At the table next to us	3	_____
there were two guys from our class. One of them was really	4	_____
funny. He tried to imitate all the people in the pizzeria.	5	_____
We couldn't stop laughing.		
But there were some the customers who did not	6	_____
like the fact that two boys were imitating them. They	7	_____
complained to the owner of the restaurant and he came over and	8	_____
told them to stop. It was a real pity because Linda and I were really	9	_____
having a fun!	10	_____

5 Vocabulary

Phrasal verbs with *sit*

Complete the sentences with the correct form of a phrasal verb with *sit*.

1 We had to _____ _____ the game because we didn't have our trainers.

2 It is difficult to _____ _____ a very long lecture.

3 A model needs to be patient when _____ _____ an artist.

4 My brother is very relaxed. He just _____ _____ and lets the world go by.

6 Fiction in mind

a Read the introduction and the extract from *A Matter of Chance*, by David A. Hill. Circle the correct answers, a, b, c or d.

Paul Morris's happy life in Italy changes when his wife dies suddenly. He develops an exciting relationship with Sandra, a friend at work. But all is not as it seems and Paul finds himself involved in a world of international crime and a car chase across Europe.

After two or three hundred ^{1} _____ of rain, ice, snow, wind and sun, the roof tile fell from its place down into the street of the old town and hit my wife in the middle of her head, killing her instantly.

Jacky.

What can I tell you about Jacky?

I can tell you how she looked that bright February morning when she stepped out into the new sun, as the snow was falling off all the roofs, as she went out to buy something for a dress she was making. For a special dinner – we ^{2} _____ been married for three years.

I have a film library of her in the back of my head: in the office; our first Christmas together, skiing in Scotland; the wedding; the trip ^{3} _____ France to our new home in Italy; and … and … I also have ten photographs of her that I took. Just ten out of the hundreds.

Afterwards, when I was able to, I looked through all the photos of our ^{4} _____ together and carefully chose the ten I liked best. I then had them enlarged, and put them in a special photo album. Which I have never opened since. ^{5} _____ this was many years ago. I am an old man now.

An old man full of memories, and full of thoughts about what could have ^{6} _____ . An old man who often thinks about the way that one tiny chance happening can change someone's life: the roof tile falls a second earlier or a second later, she goes towards a different shop, she goes towards the same shop a different way, she meets a friend and stops to talk, she doesn't meet a friend and stop to talk, the traffic lights change as she gets to the crossing … or …

Such a tiny little chance that she was there then and the roof tile was there then. Such a tiny little chance that left me, at twenty-seven years of age, ^{7} _____ in a foreign country. Italy. So much hope. Such a bright future. Such an exciting thing to do. An adventure. To go and to start a new life in Italy.

Jacky and I had met at work in Manchester. We had started at the same time. We enjoyed being together ^{8} _____ first because we were both new there, and it was good to have someone in the same situation to talk to. Talk at work led to talk in pubs, days out at weekends, and by November we were in love and planning a first skiing holiday in Scotland … the first time together, the first time away with someone I really loved.

	a	b	c	d
1	(years)	moments	stories	places
2	were	has	have	had
3	behind	to	in front of	across
4	money	life	friends	car
5	All	Each	Every	None
6	be	thought	been	fallen
7	hungry	immediately	behind	alone
8	at	from	on	in

b Read the extract again and answer the questions.

1 What was the name of the narrator's wife? _____

2 a Where was the narrator's wife killed? _____

   b Why had the narrator and his wife gone there? _____

3 How was she killed? _____

4 How old was the narrator when his wife was killed? _____

This extract is the beginning of the story. If you want to know how it continues, read the story!

Skills in mind

7 Listen

🔊 Listen to an interview with a psychologist about why people like frightening stories and the effect such stories can have on people. What does the psychologist say? Take notes to complete the sentences.

1 People like telling frightening stories so they can _____ *entertain others.* _____

2 Most of the stories have a _____

_____ .

3 If a story has comic relief, we _____ .

4 Healthy adult people are not harmed by listening to frightening stories because _____

_____ .

5 Fairy tales are important for children because _____

_____ .

6 A child who listens to fairy tales also _____

_____ .

7 Some horror films are _____ .

Listening tip

Note taking

- Before you listen, first read the task carefully. It gives you important information about what to expect in the listening. Then read through the questions. You may want to underline key words in the questions. Look at the instructions for Exercise 7. What are the key words?

- Try to predict what kinds of answers you are expected to give. Does the question ask for some specific information (for example, a person's age, or physical appearance)? What kind of language might you need to answer the question?

- Listen carefully to the information given.

- Write clear answers that are not too long, but have all the necessary information. Use abbreviations (16 instead of sixteen, km instead of kilometres).

- Keep calm if you can't answer each question immediately. If you can't answer a question, leave it out. Try to complete the missing answer during the second listening.

Unit check

1 Fill in the spaces

Complete the text with the words in the box.

| who | which | impolite | sat out | ~~usual~~ | illegal | seems | leave |

At first we thought it was the [1] _____usual_____ problem with Daniel, [2] _____ was rather unreliable. He had apparently [3] _____ the football match, [4] _____ took place every Sunday morning. Ken and I decided to go to Daniel's house the next day. When we rang the doorbell, a strange man appeared and tried to turn us away. He was rather [5] _____ . We didn't want to [6] _____ and said we wanted to see Daniel. He looked at us in a strange way and asked us to come in, but we were a little scared, so we turned and ran away. We went to the police and said we thought there might be something [7] _____ going on at Daniel's house. A police officer came back with us. When we rang the doorbell, Daniel's mother opened the door. It [8] _____ that the strange man was Daniel's grandfather!

> 9

2 Choose the correct answers

Circle the correct answers, a, b or c.

1 I love Italy, _____ you get great ice cream!
  a *where* b who c which

2 My sister works as _____ in Paris.
  a lawyer b a lawyer c the lawyer

3 Prague, _____ is the capital of the Czech Republic, is a great city.
  a where b who c which

4 This is the person _____ car was stolen.
  a that b who c whose

5 What's the name of the film _____ you saw?
  a that b where c who

6 Elvis Presley, _____ lived in Graceland, was a rock and roll legend.
  a where b who c which

7 My parents always go to _____ early in the morning.
  a the work b a work c work

8 Tolkien hated _____ he got from his fans.
  a the attention b an attention
  c attention

9 It was difficult to _____ such a boring film .
  a sit through b sit back c sit out

> 8

3 Correct the mistakes

In each sentence there is a mistake with a relative clause, an article or a phrasal verb with *sit*. Underline the mistakes and write the correct sentence.

1 Paul <u>McCartney who</u> was one of The <u>Beatles has</u> a new album.
  Paul McCartney, who was one of The Beatles, has a new album.

2 She is in Paris where she is studying Medicine. _____

3 Shall we have a look on Internet? _____

4 His father is policeman. _____

5 I love animals, especially the dogs. _____

6 He sat through to watch the film. _____

7 Can you see that man which is trying to cross the street? _____

8 Colin Campbell, that wrote *Lady in White*, is a very good writer. _____

9 The Queen sat out nine hours while the artist painted her picture. _____

> 8

How did you do?

Total: [25]

| ☺ | Very good 20 – 25 | ☺ | OK 14 – 19 | ☹ | Review Unit 15 again 0 – 13 |

16 Happiness

1 Grammar

be used to doing (something)

Match the two parts of the sentences. Then match the sentences with the pictures. Write 1–6 in the boxes.

1 I'm not used to getting up early,
2 We have to wear a uniform in our new school,
3 All the shops close at lunch time here
4 My little sister was sick,
5 My dad doesn't like his new office
6 Can I have a knife and fork please?

a and I don't like it because I'm used to wearing what I like.
b so I'm still really tired in the mornings.
c I'm not used to eating with chopsticks.
d because she's not used to travelling in the car.
e but I'm used to everything staying open all the time.
f because he's used to working from home.

2 Grammar

used to doing vs. *used to do*

a Complete the sentences. Use the correct form of *used to* and a verb from the box.

| ~~drive~~ eat laugh play speak wear |

1 My father *used to drive* a big, old, black Ford.
2 I _____ at his jokes, but now I think he's just stupid.
3 My mother _____ Spanish, but she's forgotten nearly all of it now.
4 _____ you _____ short trousers when you were a little boy?
5 My sister and I _____ video games together, but now she's left home.
6 I _____ fast food, but now I eat it all the time!

b *be used to (doing)* or *used to (do)*? Complete the sentences with the correct form of the verbs.

1 When I was younger, I used to _____ (speak) French, but I've forgotten it all.
2 I'm used to _____ (get) lots of emails every day.
3 A: This coffee is very strong.
   B: No problem. I'm used to _____ (drink) strong coffee.
4 They didn't use to _____ (care) about what other people think of them.
5 He used to _____ (live) in a houseboat on the river Seine, but he had to sell the boat.
6 She used to _____ (run) for an hour every day, but she can't any more because of a problem with her knee.
7 Are you used to _____ (live) in Britain now, or do you still find it strange?
8 When he was young, he used to _____ (be) poor, but now he's rich and he's used to _____ (buy) anything he wants!

3 Vocabulary

feel

Paul wrote about his feelings in his computer diary. Read his diary entry and complete it.
Circle the correct answers, a, b, c or d.

About five years ago, my favourite song was *I Feel Fine* by The Beatles. It feels [1] _____ to say now
that I <u>am</u> in love, I sometimes feel rather [2] _____ . For example, I feel a bit guilty because I know
that many other people are feeling [3] _____ while I'm in love. I really feel [4] _____ them.
When I walk along the street with my girlfriend, I also feel a bit [5] _____ . It seems all the world is
looking at us! A week ago I felt [6] _____ to talk to my older brother about my problems. He says
I should just feel [7] _____ that I will grow up. What does that mean? I am grown up. I'm just not
feeling [8] _____ enough to walk around holding hands with someone with other people staring
at us! Oh, dear! I'm feeling [9] _____ – I'm so glad nobody can read this.

1	a	up to	b	(strange)	c	cold	d	scared
2	a	sorry for	b	up to	c	the need	d	strange
3	a	up to	b	fine	c	lonely	d	comfortable
4	a	sorry for	b	confident	c	fine	d	stupid
5	a	cold	b	up to	c	strange	d	fine
6	a	the need	b	cold	c	weird	d	lonely
7	a	the need	b	sorry for	c	confident	d	up to
8	a	confident	b	fine	c	up to	d	the need
9	a	the need	b	fine	c	cold	d	stupid

4 Grammar

Phrasal verbs

a) Complete each sentence with the correct form of one of the phrasal verbs in brackets.

1 We have a problem, but I'm sure we can _____*work*_____ it _____*out*_____ . (work out / pick up)

2 I _____ Nick the other day when I was in Oxford Street. (give up / bump into)

3 They didn't talk to each other for a year, but they have _____ their problems _____ now. (sort out / take after)

4 He really _____ his mother's side of the family. (give up / take after)

5 We really cannot _____ his behaviour any more! (put up / put up with)

6 We have to tell them the truth, we cannot just _____ something _____ . (make up / give up)

7 This car is really old. I hope it's not going to _____ . (give up / break down)

8 Let's _____ them _____ . Maybe they'll come along! (call up / make up)

b) Put the words in order to make sentences.

1 you / to / up / doesn't / look / He
   He doesn't look up to you.

2 ran / He / from / away / her
   _____
   _____

3 each / well / other / We / on / get / with
   _____
   _____

4 our / forward / look / We / to / holidays
   _____
   _____

5 put / for / night / the / can / We / up / him
   _____
   _____

5 Pronunciation

Stress in phrasal verbs

a) 🔊 Listen and ⟨circle⟩ the prepositions that are weak. <u>Underline</u> the prepositions that are stressed.

1 a I think we can work it <u>out</u>.
  b He didn't say a word and ran ⟨out⟩ of the house.

2 a Pick your coat up.
  b She picked up her pen.

3 a I've given up sweets.
  b I've given them up.

4 a The plane took off.
  b He took off his shoes.

b) 🔊 Listen again, check and repeat.

6 Vocabulary

Expressions with prepositions

a) Match the expressions with the definitions.

1 be up and about
2 be up and down
3 be on the up-and-up
4 go on and on about something
5 be in and out of somewhere

a sometimes successful or happy and sometimes unsuccessful or unhappy

b improve continuously

c talk a lot about something in an annoying way

d recover from an illness and be able to get out of bed and move around again

e be frequently staying and receiving treatment in a particular place

b) Complete the dialogues with the expressions in Exercise 6a.

1 A: How's your father?
  B: Not too bad. I'm sure he'll _____ again soon.

2 A: I'll never be able to pass my test. It's impossible!
  B: All you do is _____ about your driving test! It's so boring.

3 A: I have never heard this band before. They play great music.
  B: Haven't you? They _____ and will have a number one hit soon!

4 A: She had a bad accident, didn't she?
  B: Yes. She's been _____ of hospital for almost a year.

5 A: How have you been?
  B: Well, thing's have been a bit _____ recently, but I hope it's going to get better with my new job.

7 Culture in mind

a Read Dido's biography. Some of the lines of the text have an extra, unnecessary word. Write the word at the end of the line. If the line is correct, put a tick (✓).

Dido

Florian Cloud de Bounevialle Armstrong, ~~was~~ called Dido, was born   1   *was*
on December 25, 1971. She entered London's Guildhall School of   2   ✓
Music at age six and mastered recorder, piano and violin by the   3   ....
time she reached her teens. Dido attended law school and did   4   ....
worked as a literary agent, while she was been singing in a series of   5   ....
local groups. Her older brother Rollo, the well-known the DJ and   6   ....
musical producer, wasn't convinced she was going to be successful, and he   7   ....
advised her not to give up her day job. But finally he changed his mind.   8   ....
Dido was appeared on his band's first album in 1995.   9   ....

For the next two years Dido toured with Rollo's band Faithless. Back in   10   ....
London, she could recorded her own demos.   11   ....

In 1997 Arista Records heard demos of Dido's songs, including *My*   12   ....
Lover's Gone, and they invited her to meet Clive Davis, the man   13   ....
responsible for finding a talent like Janis Joplin, Whitney Houston and   14   ....
Santana. The meeting was a success and led to the release of her 1999   15   ....
debut *No Angel.* Eminem borrowed part of Dido's her song *Thank You*   16   ....
for his hit *Stan.* Dido she became a star.   17   ....

b Read the text again. Mark *T* (true) or *F* (false).

1   Dido was a very musical child.

2   Dido became a musician and did not learn to do any other job.

3   Dido sang in her brother Rollo's band, Faithless.

4   After meeting Clive Davis, Dido released her album *No Angel* in 1998.

c 🔊 Two friends are talking about a Dido video. Listen and tick (✓) the correct answers.

1   Kevin and Carolyn are talking about the video for
   A   *My Life*
   B   *Take My Hand*
   C   *Thank You*

2   The website that Carolyn checked out was about mistakes
   A   in videos
   B   in song lyrics
   C   on CDs

3   The first mistake is about a hairdryer that
   A   disappears and appears again
   B   starts burning
   C   doesn't work

4   The second mistake is about an umbrella that
   A   changes its colour
   B   changes its shape
   C   changes its size

Skills in mind

8 Write

(a) Read Joanne's composition about family life. Complete her text with the correct statements (a–f). There is one statement you won't use.

a However, it is also true that things are not always easy.

b On balance, how would I respond if I were asked if I wanted to leave home?

c Personally, I would not want to be on my own too soon.

d I would love to be totally independent.

e Many of my friends would love to be independent from their parents as soon as possible.

f It's great to be part of a happy family.

'Happiness is having a large, loving, caring family in another city.'
Discuss this statement and give your own opinion.

1 _____ It is fun to be with people who like you. It is good to feel the warmth and the love of the ones who care for you. It is fantastic when you can turn to them when you have problems.

2 _____ Young people want to develop their own personality. Parents often think they know better. They find it difficult to accept that their son or their daughter wants to live and to think differently from how they used to think when they were young themselves. Consequently, young people are often frustrated and believe their parents do not understand them.

3 _____ They would love to have their own place where they can live the life they imagine must be ideal. They think that not having a parent who tells them to tidy up their room or get up at a certain time must be paradise.

4 _____ First of all, there is the financial situation. Having your own flat costs a lot of money. Secondly, being completely on your own also means a lot of responsibility. For example, I admit I like to be reminded occasionally of urgent things I have forgotten to do (although I would never admit that to my parents!). And thirdly, if members of a family accept that everybody is an individual and needs a certain amount of freedom, life in a family can be great fun.

5 _____ I would say that I am happy living with my family for now and I'll wait.

Writing tip

Developing a discursive composition (2)

- In order to make your points clearly and effectively, develop a clear progression of your argument.

- Decide how to introduce the topic, how to organise your ideas into paragraphs and how to conclude.

- Build each of your paragraphs around one particular point or idea. One effective way of doing this is to start each individual paragraph with a general statement (often called a *topic sentence*) to introduce the main idea of the paragraph. Add further sentences to support the idea.

(b) Write a composition of about 300 words to discuss the following statement and give your own opinion:

'The only way to happiness is by helping others.'

Unit check

1 Fill in the spaces

Complete the text with the words in the box.

> ~~put me up~~   strange   feel   puts up with   stupid   takes after   look up to
> sorry   used to   going on and on

My old friend, Anna, who's 18, lives in London with her family and last month they [1] ___put me up___ for a night. Anna has five younger brothers and sisters, the youngest two are only five and six, and her house is complete chaos! I'm [2] _____ living with only my parents and older brother, so it felt [3] _____ at first. I feel a bit [4] _____ for her – I really don't know how she [5] _____ all the noise! But it's obvious that her two younger sisters [6] _____ her. They even copy the way she dresses and talks! I met her parents, too, and they're really nice. She [7] _____ her mum, but when I mentioned this Anna told me people are always [8] _____ about it, so I felt a bit [9] _____ and wished I hadn't said anything! Although it wasn't very relaxing, I enjoyed staying there, as the whole family made me [10] _____ very comfortable.

9

2 Choose the correct answers

Circle the correct answers, a, b or c.

1 When I was younger, I _____ speak Spanish.
  a used to   b was used to   c 'm used to

2 I'm used to _____ late.
  a stay up   b staying up   c stayed

3 I was _____ of hospital for some time.
  a on and off   b up and about   c in and out

4 He _____ into her at a party after not seeing her for years.
  a crashed   b bumped   c danced

5 I don't mind helping him. I'm used to _____ for others.
  a care   b caring   c caring about

6 I _____ to eat vegetables, but now I eat a lot.
  a didn't use   b didn't used   c used

7 He always feels cold because he is used to _____ in a warmer country.
  a live   b living   c lives

8 I shouldn't have done it. I'm really feeling _____ !
  a up to   b fine   c guilty now

9 He doesn't feel _____ his new job.
  a on to   b up to   c down to

8

3 Correct the mistakes

In each sentence there is a mistake with expressions with *feel*, *used to*, *be used to* or a phrasal verb. Underline the mistakes and write the correct sentence.

1 I feel <u>comfortable</u> that we are going to be successful. *I feel confident that we are going to be successful.*

2 He had no friends and so he felt very lone. _____

3 We used to going to discos a lot, but now we're too old! _____

4 I'm not used to be eating so much. _____

5 I picked a bit of Spanish when I lived in Madrid. _____

6 There's no way I'm going to put with this up! _____

7 I really take from my father, we look almost the same. _____

8 I think she up made that story. _____

9 She didn't feel need to explain what she was doing. _____

8

How did you do?

Total: [25]

| 😊 Very good 20 – 25 | 😐 OK 14 – 19 | 🙁 Review Unit 16 again 0 – 13 |

Grammar reference

Unit 1

Present simple and present continuous

1 We use the present simple to talk about people's regular habits.
   *What **do** you **do** on a rainy day?*
   *Nobody in our class **smokes**.*
   *A lot of people **don't do** any exercise.*

2 We also use the present simple to talk about 'facts'; things that are always true.
   ***Do** you **have** the Internet at home?*
   *We **don't live** with our father.*
   *The school term **finishes** in June.*

3 We use the present continuous for actions or temporary situations happening at or around the moment of speaking.
   *How much money **are** you **spending** these days?*
   ***Is** your sister **working** at the moment?*
   *I'**m having** a shower right now.*

4 We also use the present continuous to talk about changing situations or trends.
   *More and more people **are going** to university.*
   *School-leavers **are finding** it harder to get a good job.*
   ***Are** boys **spending** more than girls these days?*

5 Verbs of opinion are normally used in the simple form. For example, *think, like, prefer*.
   *What **do** you **think** of the class?*
   *I **don't like** this food.*
   *I **prefer** water to fizzy drinks.*

Present perfect simple with *for* and *since*

We can use the present perfect simple to talk about actions in a period of time that started in the past and continues to the present, with *for* or *since*. It answers the question *How long ...?*

1 We use *since* to talk about the start of the time period.
   *My life has changed a lot **since I moved here**.*
   *I haven't seen her **since last weekend**.*

2 We use *for* to talk about the length of the time period.
   *We haven't been to the cinema **for weeks**.*
   *You haven't eaten meat **for as long as I can remember**.*

Present perfect simple with *just, already, yet* and *still*

We often add these words to the present perfect for emphasis.

1 We use *just* before the past participle to say that something happened a short time ago.
   *We'**ve just arrived**.*
   *They'**ve just gone** out.*

2 We use *already* at the end of the sentence or before the past participle to express surprise or emphasise that something happened.
   ***Have** you **finished already**?*
   *We'**ve already seen** this film.*

3 We use *yet at* the end of negative sentences to emphasise that something didn't happen (but probably will in the future), and at the end of questions.
*I **haven't started** this exercise **yet**. (but I will)*
***Have** you **met** my new boyfriend **yet**?*

4 We use *still* before *haven't* in negative sentences, or before *not* in questions, to show surprise that something you expected to happen didn't happen.
*I can't believe you **still haven't said** sorry.*
***Has** she **still not told** you the truth?*

Unit 2

Past simple vs. present perfect simple

1 We use the past simple to talk about complete events which are finished, or before 'now', the moment of speaking.
*I **called** you yesterday. Where **were** you?*
*We **didn't have** computers when I **was** born.*

2 We use the present perfect simple to connect the past and 'now', the moment of speaking.
*We'**ve called** you three times today. Where **have** you **been**?*
*We'**ve lived** in the same house all our lives.*

3 We use different time expressions with the past simple and the present perfect.
Use the past simple with *ten minutes ago, yesterday, last week, when I was … etc.*
We often use *for, since, just, already, yet, ever* and *never* with the present perfect.

*They **went** out a few minutes **ago**.*	*They'**ve just left**.*
*I **saw** that film **yesterday**.*	*I'**ve already seen** that film.*
*I **met** her boyfriend **last weekend**.*	*I'**ve never met** your girlfriend.*
*We **moved** there **when I was young**.*	*We'**ve lived** there **since I was a child**.*

Unit 3

Past simple vs. past continuous

1 We use the past simple to talk about actions that happened at one moment in time in the past. We use the past continuous to describe the background actions in progress around that time in the past.

*I **was playing** football. (background)*	*I **broke** my leg. (action)*
*We **were having** a picnic. (background)*	*It **started** to rain. (action)*
*What **were** you **doing**? (background)*	*I **called** you. (action)*
*I **wasn't paying** attention. (background)*	*I **got** hit by a car. (action)*

2 It is common to use *when* with the past simple to introduce the past action, or *while* with the past continuous to introduce the background.
*I broke my leg **while** I **was playing** football.*
*We were having a picnic **when** it **started** to rain.*
*What were you doing **when** I **called** you?*
***While** I **wasn't paying** attention, I got hit by a car.*

3 Other time words that we use with the past simple are *then* and *as soon as*. We can also use *as* with the same meaning as *while*.
***As soon as** I **got** home, I turned on the TV for the big game.*
*The picture came on, **then** I **learned** the bad news.*
*Someone scored **as** I **was making** a sandwich.*

Past simple vs. past perfect

1   We use the past simple to talk about an event that happened at a specific time in the past.
We use the past perfect when we need to emphasise that one event happened <u>before</u> another.
*The match **had started** when we **got** there.*
*When I **got** to the street I **realised** I **hadn't brought** his address with me.*
*I **knew** we'd **met** before somewhere.*
*How long **had** you **been** there when they finally **arrived**?*

2   Sometimes it is necessary to use the past perfect to make the meaning clear.
*She'd **left** when I got there. (I didn't see her.)*
*She **left** when I got there (but I saw her).*
*I went to the party. There **was** food there (and it was delicious).*
*I went to the party. There **had been** food there (but I was too late to get some).*

3   It is not necessary to use the past perfect when *before* or *after* is used.
*She left **before** I got there.*

4   It is wrong to use the past perfect when a story is told in the same order as the events happened.
*I **went** in, **said** hello, and **left** straight away.*
but
*I **went** back inside because I'd **forgotten** to say goodbye to some people.*

Unit 4

Present perfect simple vs. present perfect continuous

1   We use the present perfect simple to emphasise the result or completion of an activity.
*I've **copied** that CD you asked me for. Here it is.*
*I've **bought** everybody's presents. Aren't I organised!*

We use the present perfect continuous to emphasise the activity, not the result or completion
of the activity (it may not be finished).
*I've **been copying** CD's all morning. Great fun!*
*I've **been shopping** for presents. That's why I wasn't here.*

2   We use the present perfect simple to emphasise 'how many'.
*I've **done** ten exercises this morning.*
*You've **had** three pieces of cake already!*
*How many sandwiches **have** you **made**?*

We use the present perfect continuous to emphasise 'how long'.
*I've **been doing** exercises for hours.*
*You've **been eating** cake since you got here!*
*How long **have** you **been making** sandwiches?*

3   Remember that some verbs express a 'state', and are not normally used in the continuous form.
*I've always **loved** you.* (NOT ~~I've always been loving~~ ...)
*We've never **had** a big, expensive car.* (NOT ~~We've never been having~~ ...)

should / ought to / had better

We use *should* or *ought to* to give advice, or say what we think is a good (or bad) idea. They have the same meaning. Remember, *should* is a modal verb, and is used without *to*. We use *had better* to give stronger advice or warnings. The form is always past (never ~~have~~ better), but the meaning is present. *Had better* is also used without *to*.

*You **should** take a rest.*   *You **shouldn't** worry so much.*
*She **ought to** be more careful.*   *She **ought not to** be so pessimistic.*
*He'd **better** start doing some work.*   *He'd **better not** come near me.*

Unit 5

Future review

There are three common ways of talking about the future in English.

1   When we want to talk about our <u>intentions</u>, or to talk about a <u>process</u> that has started and will end in the future, we use *be going to*.

   There's a test tomorrow, so I'm going to revise for it tonight. (intention)

   I feel awful! I think I'm going to be sick. (process)

   I didn't like their last CD, so I'm not going to buy their new one. (intention)

   We aren't going to watch the match tonight. (intention)

2   When we want to talk about <u>arrangements</u> for the future, we use the present continuous (we almost never use this in the negative).

   My sister's seeing the dentist tomorrow morning.

   I'm having lunch with some friends on Saturday.

   My grandfather is retiring next month.

3   When we want to make <u>predictions</u> about the future, we use *will / will not (won't)*.

   Take this medicine, and then you'll feel a lot better.

   The weather forecast says that next winter there'll be lots of snow here.

   He hasn't done much work - I'm sure he won't pass the test.

   My team are playing the champions tomorrow, so they probably won't win.

Unit 6

Predictions with *will, might* and *be likely to*

The chance of something happening	100% ↑ ↓ 0%	will	
		will probably	is likely to
		might	might not
		probably won't	isn't likely to
		won't	

When we make predictions about the future, we can use *will*, *might* and *be likely to* (and their negative forms) to show how sure we are about the chances of something happening.

My parents will be really angry when I get home tonight. (100% sure)

My father will probably / is likely to shout at me.

They might not let me go out again next weekend.

My brother probably won't / isn't likely to help me.

But next weekend, my parents won't remember what happened!

First conditional with *if* and *unless*

In first conditional sentences:

a   both verbs refer to actions or events in the future;

b   the verb tense after the words *if* or *unless* is present simple;

c   the verb tense in the other clause is *will* or *won't*;

d   we can use *if* or *unless* (which means 'if not');

e   when we use *unless*, the verb that follows is in the positive.

For example:
> *If my friends **visit** me (tomorrow), we'**ll go** out for lunch.*
> *I'**ll take** them to the Chinese restaurant, unless they **want** to eat pizza.*
> *(= .... if they **don't want** to eat pizza.)*
> *Unless my parents give me some money, I **won't be able** to pay. (= If my parents **don't give** .....)*

Unit 7

Present and past passive review

We form the passive with a form of the verb *to be* + the **past participle** of the main verb.
> *English **is spoken** all over the world.*
> *My bike **was stolen** last night.*

The present perfect passive

We form the present perfect passive with *have/has been* + past participle.
> *Our old house isn't there any more - it'**s been pulled** down.*
> *The rules of tennis **haven't been changed** for a long time.*

The future passive

We form the future passive with *will be / won't be* + past participle.
> *Those trees **will be cut** down next month.*
> *If you don't behave properly, you **won't be invited** again!*

Causative *have (have something done)*

1   This structure has the form *have* + noun + past participle.
> *I'm taking my camera to the shop. I'm going to **have it repaired**.*

2   We use *have something done* when we talk about a service or function that someone else does for us.
> *I **had my hair cut** last week. (= I went to a hairdresser and a person cut my hair.)*
> *My grandparents want to **have their house painted**. (= They want to pay a painter to paint their house.)*
> *We'**ve had our car repaired**. (= We've taken our car to a garage and someone has repaired it for us. Now it's OK again.)*

Unit 8

make / let / be allowed to

1   We use *make* [*someone do*] to talk about an obligation.
> *Our teacher **makes us do** a lot of homework. (= We cannot choose, it's an obligation that our teacher gives us.)*
> *My older brother **made me lend** him some money. (= I could not choose, my brother forced me.)*

2   We use *let* [*someone do*] to talk about permission.
> *Our teacher **lets us leave** early on Fridays. (= The teacher gives us permission to leave early.)*
> *My father **let me use** the car yesterday. (= My father gave me permission to use the car.)*

3   We use *be allowed to* [*do something*] to say that someone has (or has not) got permission.
> *At our school, we'**re allowed to wear** jeans if we want to.*
> *When we were young, we **weren't allowed to play** outside in the street.*
> *You'**re not allowed to park** here.*

Modals of obligation, prohibition and permission review

We can also use verbs, including modal verbs, to talk about permission and obligation.

1   *have to / don't have to* is used to talk about obligation / no obligation.

   I **have to get up** at six o'clock every day. (= This is an obligation for me.)

   We **don't have to wear** school uniform. (= Wearing school uniform is not an obligation for us.)

   My sister **had to go** to work last Sunday. (= This was an obligation for my sister.)

   We **didn't have to pay** for the meal. (= It was not necessary to pay.)

2   *can / can't* is used to talk about permission.

   You **can watch** TV if you want to. (= I give you permission to watch TV.)

   We **can't go** in because we're not 18. (= We don't have permission to go in.)

3   We use *mustn't* to prohibit someone from doing something, or to say that something is very important.

   You **mustn't forget** to take your medicine. (= It is very important not to forget.)

   We **mustn't be** late! (= It is very important for us not to be late.)

   You **mustn't talk** to me like that! (= I am telling you that I don't allow this.)

Unit 9

Verbs with gerunds; and infinitives

1   When a verb is followed by another verb, the second verb is either in the gerund (*-ing*) or infinitive form. The form of the second verb depends on the first verb.

2   Some verbs (e.g. *enjoy, detest, (don't) mind, imagine, feel like, suggest, practise, miss*) are followed by a verb in the gerund form.

   I don't **enjoy living** in the city very much.

   She doesn't **feel like going** out tonight.

3   Other verbs (e.g. *hope, promise, ask, learn, expect, decide, afford, offer, choose*) are followed by a verb in the infinitive form.

   We can't **afford to go** on holiday this year.

   I **promise to pay** you on Monday.

Verbs with gerunds and infinitives

1   Some verbs (e.g. *remember, stop, try*) can be followed by a second verb in either the gerund or infinitive form. The form of the second verb depends on the meaning of the sentence.

Remember

   I **remember going** to my first football match with my dad. (= I remember the occasion.)

   I **remembered to go** to the stadium and buy the tickets. (= I promised my son I would buy the tickets and I didn't forget to do this.)

Stop

   I **stopped to watch** the news headlines. (= I was doing something (my homework / talking to my parents) when the news started. I stopped the first activity because I wanted to watch the headlines.)

   I **stopped watching** TV and went to bed. (= I was watching TV. I was tired so I turned off the TV and went to bed.)

2   Some verbs (e.g. *like, love, hate, prefer, begin, start*) can be followed by gerund or infinitive with no difference in meaning.

   We **began to run** when it **started raining**.

   We **began running** when it **started to rain**.

Unit 10

Second conditional

1 When we want to talk about imaginary actions and their consequences, we use the second conditional.

2 The second conditional has two clauses; 'if + the past tense' to introduce the hypothetical situation and 'would / could / might + verb' to talk about the imaginary result.

   *If I **had** more time, I **would learn** the guitar.*

3 The clauses can be put the other way around. In this case we don't use a comma.

   *She **would be** the best student if she **worked** harder.*

4 Other ways of saying *if* in a second conditional include *what if, suppose, imagine* and *say*.

   ***What if** you won the lottery? Would you be happy?*

   ***Suppose** you could live forever. Would you want to?*

   ***Imagine** you knew your brother was a burglar. Would you tell the police?*

   ***Say** you could live anywhere. Where would you choose?*

I wish / if only + past simple

1 When we want to talk about how we would like our present life to be different, we can use *wish* or *if only* + past simple.

2 Although we are talking about our present situation, *wish / if only* are followed by the past tense.

   *I wish I **didn't have** so much homework.*

   *Dave wishes he **had** a girlfriend.*

3 We use *wish / if only + could* when we want to talk about having the ability or permission to do something.

   *I wish I **could** play the guitar.*

   *Sally wishes she **could** go to the party.*

Unit 11

Linkers of contrast

1 When we want to introduce a contrast, we use words like *however, although, even though, in spite of, despite* and *whereas*.

2 *Despite* and *in spite of* are followed by a noun or verb in the gerund form.

   ***Despite being** very rich, he's not happy.*

   ***In spite of his wealth**, he's not very happy.*

3 *Although* and *even though* are followed by a clause.

   ***Although** they played badly, they still won.*

   ***Even though** he's lived in Paris for three years, he doesn't speak French.*

4 *However* always starts a new sentence.

   *I don't usually like action films. **However**, I really enjoyed Troy.*

5 *Whereas* contrasts two different subjects. It can come at the beginning or in the middle of the sentence.

   *The beaches in the north are always crowded, **whereas** the beaches in the south are usually quiet.*

Modals of deduction (present)

1 To make a guess about a present situation, we can use the modal verbs *can't, must, might* and *could*.

2 When we are sure something is true, we use *must*.
   *She got ten valentine cards. She **must** be popular.*

3 When we are sure something is <u>not</u> true, we use *can't*.
   *He's failed the driving test five times. He **can't** be a very good driver.*

4 When we think there is a possibility something is true, we use *might* or *could*.
   *They're speaking Spanish so they **might** be Mexican.*
   *They **could** be brother and sister. They look quite similar.*

Unit 12
Indirect questions

1 After expressions like *I don't understand ..., I wonder ..., I want to know ... and I don't know ...* we often find question words. However, what comes after the question word is not a question, and does not follow the word order for questions.
   *I wonder **why she said that**.* (**NOT** *I wonder why ~~did she say that~~.*)
   *I don't know **when we will arrive**.* (**NOT** *I don't know when ~~will we arrive~~.*)
   *I want to know **where you're going**.* (**NOT** *I want to know where ~~are you going~~.*)

2 If we want to ask less direct questions, we can use an expression such as *Can you tell me ...,* *Do you happen to know ...* and *Do you know ...* . This is the question, so what comes after these expressions does not follow the word order for questions.
   *Can you tell me **where the toilets are**?* (**NOT** *Can you tell me where ~~are the toilets?~~*)
   *Do you happen to know **if he's French**?* (**NOT** *Do you happen to know ~~is he French?~~*)
   *Do you know why **she left early**?* (**NOT** *Do you know why ~~did she leave early?~~*)

Modals of deduction (past)

To make a guess about a past situation, we can use the modal verbs *can't, must, might* and *could* with the present perfect tense.
*You were all alone in the house. You **must have been** really scared.*
*I'm not sure how the vase got broken but it **might have been** the dog.*
*Police believe that the criminal **could have left** the country.*
*It **can't have been** my husband. He was at home with me all last night.*

Unit 13
Reported statements review

In reported speech, we often change the verb that was used in direct speech.

'It's late,' he said.	➡ *He said it **was** late.*
*'I **'ve lost** my watch,' she said.*	➡ *She said she**'d lost** her watch.*
*'We **didn't enjoy** our holiday,' they said.*	➡ *They said they **hadn't enjoyed** their holiday.*
*'I **can't open** the door,' my sister said.*	➡ *My sister said she **couldn't open** the door.*
*'I**'ll pick** you up at eight,' she said.*	➡ *She said she**'d pick** me up at eight.*

Reported questions review

1 With reported questions, we use statement word order and **NOT** question word order.
   *They asked us **where the station was**.* (**NOT** *They asked us ~~where was the station.~~*)
   *I asked him **what we could do**.* (**NOT** *I asked him ~~what could we do.~~*)
   *She asked me **where I lived**.* (**NOT** *She asked me ~~where did I live.~~*)

2   When we report yes/no questions, we use *if* (or *whether*) and statement word order.

    'Is London very big?'   ➡   *He asked me **if** London was big.*

    'Do you play chess?'   ➡   *She asked me **whether** I played chess.*

    'Did your father go abroad last year?' ➡   *He asked me **if** my father had gone abroad last year.*

3   When we report *wh-* questions (with *who / where / what / how / when* etc.), we use the same question word and statement word order.

    *'**Who** are you talking to?'*   ➡   *He asked me **who** I was talking to.*

    *'**When** did you arrive?'*   ➡   *They asked me **when** I had arrived.*

    *'**How much** money have you got?'* ➡   *She asked me **how much** money I'd got.*

4   With requests, we use *'asked'* + person + *to* (do).

    'Please carry this for me, Mike.'   ➡   *She **asked Mike to carry** it for her.*

    'Can you open the window please?' ➡   *He **asked me to open** the window.*

    'Please don't be late!'   ➡   *The teacher **asked us not to be** late.*

Reporting verb patterns

We can use many different verbs to report speech. Be careful about the pattern that follows these verbs.

1   Some verbs (e.g. *say, explain*) are followed by *that* + clause.

    *He **said that** the film was one of the best he'd ever seen.*

    *She **explained that** she couldn't come because she had work to do.*

2   Some verbs (e.g. *offer, refuse, agree*) are followed by the infinitive with *to*.

    *My mother **offered to lend** me some money.*

    *She **refused to tell** me her name.*

    *I **agreed to go** with them.*

3   Some verbs (e.g. *ask, order, invite, tell, persuade*) are followed by an object + infinitive with *to*.

    *My father **asked my sister to help** him choose a present for my mother.*

    *The policeman **ordered them to stop**.*

    *My grandparents **invited me to have** lunch with them.*

    *Our teacher **told us to concentrate** more.*

    *My friends **persuaded me to go** to the concert with them.*

4   Some verbs (e.g. *apologise for, suggest*) are followed by a noun or a gerund.

    *He apologised for **the noise / making** a noise.*

    *She suggested **a walk / going** for a walk.*

Unit 14

Third conditional

1   We use the third conditional to speculate about how things might have been different in the past. The third conditional is formed with *If* + past perfect + *would (not) have* + past participle.

    *If we'**d waited** for you, we **would have missed** the beginning of the film.*

    (= We <u>didn't</u> wait for you, so we <u>didn't</u> miss the beginning of the film.)

    *If you **hadn't fallen asleep** in the lesson, the teacher **wouldn't have made** you stay after school.*

    (= You <u>did</u> fall asleep and the teacher <u>did</u> make you stay after school.)

2   Instead of *would*, we can use *might* (if we are not very sure of the possible result).

    *If we'**d waited** for you, we **might have missed** the beginning of the film.*

I wish / If only + past perfect simple

We use *I wish* or *If only* + past perfect to express regret about past actions or events.

    *I **wish** I'**d phoned** her. (= I <u>didn't</u> phone her, and I regret it.)*

    *I **wish** they **hadn't told** you about it. (= They <u>did</u> tell you, and I regret it.)*

If only I'd studied harder. (= I didn't study hard, and I regret it.)
If only we hadn't argued with them. (= We did argue with them, and I regret it.)

should / shouldn't have done

We use *should / shouldn't have (done)* to criticise past actions.
You should've told me. (= You didn't tell me, and I think that was wrong.)
He should've scored. (= He didn't score, and I think that was wrong.)
She shouldn't have broken my camera. (= She did break my camera, and that was wrong.)
We shouldn't have come here. (= We did come here, and I think that was wrong.)

Unit 15
Defining and non-defining relative clauses

1   We use relative clauses to add information about the subject or object of a sentence.

2   Relative clauses are introduced by words like *that, which, where, who* and *whose*.

We use *that / which* to refer to things.
*That's the car **that / which** almost killed me.*

We use *that / who* to refer to people.
*The woman **who / that** served me was American.*

We use *where* to refer to places.
*These photos were taken in Paris, **where** we went for our holiday last year.*

We use *whose* to refer to possession.
*She's the girl **whose** brother plays football for Liverpool.*

3   Sometimes the information is essential to know what exactly we are talking about. In these cases we use a defining relative clause and we don't use a comma.
*My brother **who** lives in Canada is an architect.*
(= I have more than one brother but I am talking about the one who lives in Canada.)

4   Sometimes the information is additional. We don't need it to understand what we are talking about. This is a non-defining relative clause. The extra information is included between commas. (NB In these sentences we <u>can't</u> use *that*.) For example:
*My brother, **who lives in Canada**, is an architect.*
(= I only have one brother. He lives in Canada and is an architect.)

Definite, indefinite and zero article

1   We use the definite article (*the*):

a   when something is unique.
*Have you seen **the** moon tonight? It's beautiful.*

b   to talk about the ability to play an instrument.
*She's plays **the** violin really well.*

c   to refer to specific things.
*I love **the** sound of birds singing in the morning.*

d   when we know what is being talked about.
*Have you got **the** money? (= I lent you last week.)*

2   We use the indefinite article *(a/an)*:

a   to talk about professions.
*My dad's **a** teacher.*

b   to talk about <u>a</u> not one thing.
*I read **a** really good book last week.*

3 We use the zero article (no article):

a to refer to things in general.
Music always makes me feel happy.

b to talk about places as institutions.
I go to church about twice a month.

Unit 16

be used to doing vs. *used to do*

1 When we want to say that we are accustomed or not to doing things, we can use the expressions *be used to* and *get used to*.

2 These expressions are followed by a noun or the gerund (*-ing*) form of a verb.
He's not used to being so popular.
She's not really used to young children.

3 *be used to* refers to a state.
I'm not used to working so hard.

4 *get used to* refers to the process.
It took me years to get used to driving on the left.

5 Don't confuse these expressions with *used to*, which refers to past habits and is followed by an infinitive without *to*.
We used to spend our holidays in the south of France when I was a child.

The grammar of phrasal verbs

1 Phrasal verbs have two or three parts.
Guess who I bumped into yesterday? (met by chance)
I really look up to my Maths teacher. (respect)

2 With some phrasal verbs, these parts can be separated by the object of the verb.
I called up my friend as soon as I heard the news. OR
I called my friend up as soon as I heard the news.
However, when the object is a pronoun, it must come between the two parts.
I called him up. (NOT ~~I called up him.~~)

3 In other phrasal verbs, these parts can never be separated.
I take after my mother. (NOT ~~I take my mother after.~~)

4 Three part phrasal verbs cannot be split.
I've made up with my girlfriend.

5 To find out if a phrasal verb can be split or not, look in a dictionary:
If it **can** be split, it will be listed: *call <u>sb</u> up*
If it **can't** be split, it will be listed: *take after <u>sb</u>*

6 Some phrasal verbs have more than one meaning.
My car's broken down. (stopped working)
When she heard the news, she broke down. (started crying)

Acknowledgements

The authors and publishers are grateful to the following for permission to use copyright material in *English in MInd 3 Workbook*. While every effort has been made, it has not been possible to identify the sources of all the material used and in such cases the publishers would welcome information from the copyright owners:

for the article on p. 8, 'MS Dynamite's Victory blasts mercury norms', by A. Chrisafis, published in The Guardian on 19th September 2002, © The Guardian;

for the extract on p. 19 from *Charlotte's Web* reprinted by permission of International Creative Management, Inc. and Hamish Hamilton (UK and Commonwealth) Copyright © 1952 by E.B. White;

Jania Barrell for the extract on p. 43 from *But Was it Murder* (2000) and Frank Brennan for the extract on p. 67 from 'Finders Keepers' from *The Fruitcake Special and Other Stories* (2000) and David A Hill for the extract on p. 91 from *A Matter of Chance* (1999) © Cambridge University Press, reprinted with permission of the publisher and author.

The publishers are grateful to the following for permission to reproduce photographic material:

Peter Adams Photography / Alamy for p. 71; Archivberlin Fotoagentur GmbH / Alamy for p. 7(br); Jon Arnold Images / Alamy for p. 7(bl); Associated Press for p. 31; BBC Photo Library for p. 50; Anthony Blake Picture Library for p. 7(mr); Corbis for p. 25(l); EON / Ronald Grant Archive for p. 53; foodfolio / Alamy for p. 7(ml); Getty Images for p. 4(t); Neil Holmes Freelance Digital / Alamy for p. 7(t); Image Source / Alamy for p. 6; Link Picture Library for p. 79; New Line Cinema / Ronald Grant Archive for p. 56(l); PA Photos for p. 8; Paramount Pictures / Ronald Grant Archive for p. 56(t); Penguin books for p. 19; plainpicture / Alamy for p. 55; Punchstock / Thinkstock for p. 4; Redferns Music Picture Library for pp. 23, 73(t), 97; Rex Features for pp. 25(r), 49, 56(r), 73(b); Science Photo Library for p. 32; Universal Pictures / Ronald Grant Archive for pp. 56(m), 92; Warner Bros. / Ronald Grant Archive for p. 68; Janine Wiedel photography / Alamy for p. 60; 20th Century Fox / Ronald Grant Archive for p. 80.
Commissioned photography by Gareth Boden on p. 14.

Picture Research by Kevin Brown

The publishers are grateful to the following illustrators:

Asa Anderson c/o NB Illustration pp. 16, 48, 64, 90, 95: Fred Blunt c/o Joking Apart pp. 18, 62, 70, 76: Mark Duffin pp. 40: Ferris & Lloyd Productions pp. 29, 46: Martha Gavin pp. 6, 28, 66: Ben Hasler c/o NB Illustration pp. 10, 30, 44, 54, 76, 82: Sophie Joyce pp. 12, 34, 78: Graham Kennedy pp. p5, 17, 23, 37, 49, 59, 61, 77, 80, 86, 88, 98: Brian Lee pp. 52, 74: Naf c/o Joking Apart pp 36, 42, 58, 65, 82, 83: Kath Walker pp. 22, 41, 60, 94.

The publishers are grateful to the following contributors:

Sarah Ackroyd: CD-ROM exercises
Bee2 Ltd: multimedia developer
Kevin Brown: picture research
Annie Cornford: editorial work
Pentacor Book Design: text design and layouts
Anne Rosenfeld: audio CD audio recordings

The CD-ROM photographs are from © istockphoto.com, Punchstock or taken by Cambridge University Press

CD instructions

Audio CD

Play the CD in a standard CD player, or on your computer.

CD-ROM

No installation – simply insert the disc into your CD-ROM drive and the application will start automatically. Close any media applications (for example, Microsoft® Windows Media® Player) before inserting the disc. If the application does not start automatically, browse to your CD-ROM drive and double-click the 'EIM' icon.

Audio CD track listing

TRACK	UNIT	EXERCISE	TRACK	UNIT	EXERCISE
1	Introduction		19	9	7a
2	1	3a	20	10	4
3	1	3b	21	11	2
4	2	2b	22	12	3
5	3	2b	23	12	5b
6	3	6a	24	13	7a
7	3	6b	25	13	7b
8	4	3b	26	14	4a
9	4	5b	27	14	4b
10	4	6a	28	15	2b
11	5	2a	29	15	7
12	6	5	30	16	5a
13	7	2b	31	16	7c
14	7	8	32	3	10b
15	8	3a	33	7	10b
16	8	3b	34	11	6
17	8	7c	35	15	9b
18	9	3a			

Terms and conditions of use for the English in Mind Workbook Audio CD / CD-ROM

1   Licence

(a) Cambridge University Press grants the customer the licence to use one copy of this CD-ROM (i) on a single computer for use by one or more people at different times, or (ii) by a single person on one or more computers (provided the CD-ROM is only used on one computer at one time and is only used by the customer), but not both.

(b) The customer shall not: (i) copy or authorise copying of the CD-ROM, (ii) translate the CD-ROM, (iii) reverse-engineer, disassemble or decompile the CD-ROM, (iv) transfer, sell, assign or otherwise convey any portion of the CD-ROM, or (v) operate the CD-ROM from a network or mainframe system.

2   Copyright

All material contained within the CD-ROM is protected by copyright and other intellectual property laws. The customer acquires only the right to use the CD-ROM and does not acquire any rights, express or implied, other than those expressed in the licence.

3   Liability

To the extent permitted by applicable law, Cambridge University Press is not liable for direct damages or loss of any kind resulting from the use of this product or from errors or faults contained in it and in every case Cambridge University Press' liability shall be limited to the amount actually paid by the customer for the product.

CD-ROM System Requirements:
- 800 x 600 resolution
- a mouse
- a sound card and speakers or headphones

For PC:
- Pentium 500 MHz or higher
- 256 MB RAM
- Windows 2000 or XP

For Apple Mac:
- 500 MHz processor or higher
- 256 MB RAM
- OS X 10.4